I Still Believe

Also by Kurt Bruner

Inklings of God

I Still Believe

kurtBRUNER

How Listening to Christianity's Critics
Strengthens Faith

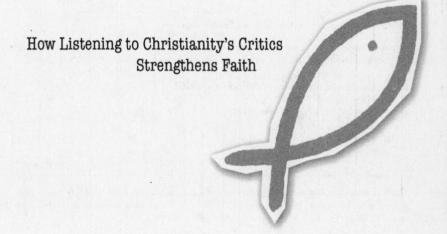

GRAND RAPIDS, MICHIGAN 49530 USA

Kurt Bruner can be contacted by email at
KurtBruner@msn.com

ZONDERVAN™

I Still Believe
Copyright © 2005 by Kurt Bruner

Requests for information should be addressed to:
Zondervan, *Grand Rapids, Michigan 49530*

Library of Congress Cataloging-in-Publication Data

Bruner, Kurt D.
   I still believe : how listening to Christianity's critics strengthens faith / Kurt Bruner.
      p. cm.
   Includes bibliographical references and index.
   ISBN-10: 0-310-24997-X
   ISBN-13: 078-0-310-24997-9
   1. Apologetics. I. Title.
   BT1103.B78   2005
   239—dc22
                                                                                    2005006092

Published in association with the literary agency of Alive Communications, Inc., 7680 Goddard Street, Suite 200, Colorado Springs, CO 80920.

Edited by Rebecca Shingledecker

Interior design by Beth Shagene

Printed in the United States of America

05 06 07 08 09 10 11 12 /❖ DCI/ 15 14 13 12 11 10 9 8 7 6 5 4 3 2 1

Contents

To my fellow Stinklings.
Thanks for pushing me
toward the sometimes unwelcome truth.

There lives more faith in honest doubt,
believe me, than in half the creeds.

<small>TENNYSON</small>

Listening to the Unconvinced

I imagine even the most die-hard believers have moments when they become uneasy about their faith. Kind of like that feeling you get when you crawl into bed and your wife asks whether you remembered to lock all of the doors. No matter how confident you may feel that the doors are properly bolted, the mere suggestion keeps you awake until you go downstairs and double check.

I've often found myself comfortably between the sheets, ready to settle into a confident faith. But then the suggestions come.

"How can you be so sure when so many are not?"

"Why do you find Christianity so appealing when others find it so offensive?"

"If most of earth's six billion people reject Christianity, isn't it arrogant to think you have the corner on truth?"

Unable to properly rest until I've double checked, I decided to explore what makes my religion so hard to accept—to grab each handle, give it a good twist, and see whether it opens or remains securely locked.

I've never experienced what you would call a serious crisis of doubt; sometimes I envy those who have. Strong faith should not accept easy answers, something I probably have done too quickly at times. Not that I don't ask hard questions or face difficult realities! It's just that I do so from the perspective of one who wholeheartedly accepts Christianity as the best description of our world and the dilemma in which we find ourselves. It also offers a unique solution, a key that fits the lock better than any other religious or secular offering.

Raised in church and immersed in religious assumptions since diapers, I suppose faith comes easier for me than for some others. As an adult, I attended a well-respected seminary where I studied theology and apologetics. Consequently, I believe in Christianity like I "believe" in the changing seasons or the law of gravity. And I find those who don't a curiosity.

Still, it bothers me that some of history's greatest minds have rejected Christian belief. Of course, just as many have not. For every Neitzsche, there is a Lewis; for every Voltaire, a Pascal; and for every Twain a Tolstoy.

A number of Christianity's most hardened opponents once counted themselves believers, while among its most articulate defenders we find former atheists and skeptics.

Clearly, something exists behind unbelief besides the reasons given. Is it genuine doubt or a defensive bluff? Sincere questioning or cynical heckling? Hard to say.

Of course, the same can be asked of Christians. We must seem a bit scary at times, overly eager to draw others into our odd little subculture. Is our motive to rescue them from eternal damnation or to prop up our own wavering confidence? Intense conviction or contrived enthusiasm? Looking from the outside, I guess it is just as hard to tell.

In order to find out, I decided to listen to the unconvinced—truly listen, not simply pause long enough to formulate my next argument. I have no interest in making my case to unbelievers; that's been done. I want to hear their case to me. Rather than attempt to overcome their objections or argue their points, I want to understand their dilemma.

What makes Christianity so hard to swallow?

Why does the faith I hold so dear repel others?

If so many sincere people doubt to the point of skepticism, then what makes me sure my own faith isn't mere wishful thinking? Perhaps I am just needy or naïve, hastily accepting a religion that billions reject. Perhaps I believe because I want it to be true. But then, maybe others don't believe because they want it to be false.

The Dynamics of Doubt

Poet Alfred Lord Tennyson said that there is more faith in honest doubt than in half the creeds. I, for one, would like to find out why. In order to do so, I dove deeply into the reasons for and the dynamics of doubt, unbelief, and skepticism. Ignoring etiquette, I discussed religion in polite company so that I could listen to the unconvinced—from the common doubts of the faithful to the nasty attacks of the hostile.

Using a journalistic approach, I've chronicled a number of face-to-face interviews with a variety of individuals, most who do not embrace Christianity despite some level of exposure to the teachings and followers of Christ. You will read their stories in their words, with only names and places changed to protect confidentiality. Folks like Ralph, the friendly skeptic; Mary Ellen, a gentle soul who misses the church she dislikes; and Ken, a child who resented being told his Muslim mommy is going to burn in hell.

I have also captured the voice of unbelief as expressed in the writings of famous unbelievers, living and dead.

Those represented have been placed in eight categories of unbelief: the disillusioned, the seeker, the offended, the apathetic, the skeptic, the heckler, the uneasy, and the rebel—an admittedly incomplete list, as others could be explored. Obviously, no individual fits neatly into any single classification. You can become a skeptic after being offended, but skepticism can also make you more prone to take offense. We are complicated beings.

I also asked long-term believers what parts of Christianity make them uneasy, studied famous skeptics to understand why they seem so on edge, and researched what some of history's great minds have said in the continuing debate over faith. What I encountered fills the pages to follow in language full of candor, brutality, and sincerity.

I invite you to sit quietly on the other side of a one-way mirror, observing the dialogue. What you see and hear may bother you (I know it did me). There may be moments when you can relate to the misgivings expressed, even hearing your own thoughts in the words of others. Other times you might feel an overwhelming urge to shout through the glass to correct mistaken impressions, to refute faulty arguments, or to justify actions of the God you adore (I felt the same temptation). But remember, our goal is not to argue, but to listen.

If you are a Christian, this book may serve as a safe way to examine some of the tough questions that drive lingering, unspoken doubt. It might also help you better understand the unbelievers in your life. Perhaps it will shed some light on questions you have about friends and loved ones:

"Why doesn't Frank seem even remotely interested in God or eternity?"

"My teenage son is questioning the Christian faith. Should I be worried?"

"Why does Aunt Betty get so defensive whenever we discuss spiritual matters?"

"My spouse doesn't believe. Am I doing something wrong?"

For those who do not embrace Christian faith—whether you abandoned it after childhood or never gave it a thought—this book may serve as an honest look in the mirror. You may find my confidence in Christianity as perplexing as I find your skepticism. Or maybe you would prefer a root canal to being confronted by a die-hard believer. I hope you find this exploration refreshingly honest as I openly discuss parts of the faith that even Christians find troubling. Perhaps this book might shore up your doubt as you listen to others articulate their reasons for rejecting Christianity, reasons you have felt but couldn't put into words. But it also might cause you to start checking your own locks.

With that, we begin our inquiry into what makes Christianity hard for so many to swallow, while others eat to their heart's content.

Chapter 1

Pester the Perishing

I grew up in a traditional evangelical church that considered saving the lost a chief aim of the Christian life. Sermons implored us to share the good news of the gospel with friends, neighbors, relatives, classmates, and anyone else with a pulse. The best evangelists even found ways to discuss Christ with grocery store clerks, somewhere between "How are you today?" and "Have a nice day."

I never quite mastered that one. I couldn't bring myself to casually ask, "If you were to die today, do you know where you would spend eternity?" while sorting double coupons.

Still, the church offered plenty of other opportunities for reaching unbelievers—like door-to-door visitation, the process of walking house-to-house throughout the community, inviting folks to church (and if you got lucky, to heaven). The moral support of going in pairs, never alone, helped a great deal, since discussing Christianity with complete strangers can seem more frightening than bungee jumping off the Golden Gate Bridge.

I remember one occasion when I was about fourteen. They partnered me with another teenage boy and sent us off into the highways and byways. Talk about scary—two guys who spent most waking hours worrying about too much acne or too few whiskers, standing before a door that would soon open. Behind the door might be anyone: a sweet old lady, a haggard mother of preschoolers, or a Hell's Angels biker. No matter who appeared,

15

however, it was our job to share the good news of the gospel with someone whose meal we had just interrupted.

It probably wasn't the most effective method of evangelism. But we did it anyway, believing the "unsaved" lived in perpetual misery even as they hurtled toward eternal damnation.

Why did we feel so motivated to share Christ? Part of the urge came from the songs we sang during Sunday services that centered around the theme of evangelism. Titles such as "Send the Light" reminded us of the urgent task to which we'd been called:

> There's a call comes ringing o'er the restless wave,
>   "Send the light! Send the light!"
> There are souls to rescue, there are souls to save,
>   Send the light! Send the light![1]

"Throw Out the Life-Line" was another favorite:

> Throw out the Life-Line! Throw out the Life-Line!
>   Someone is drifting away;
> Throw out the Life-Line! Throw out the Life-Line!
>   Someone is sinking today.[2]

But I remember one song more vividly than any other, perhaps because we sang it so often. I doubt that I can ever forget "Rescue the Perishing."

> Rescue the perishing, care for the dying,
> Snatch them in pity from sin and the grave;
> Weep o'er the erring one, lift up the fallen,
> Tell them of Jesus, the mighty to save.
> Rescue the perishing, care for the dying;
> Jesus is merciful, Jesus will save.[3]

We got the message. People living in darkness need the light. Unbelievers are like drowning men gasping for air while gulping seawater, so we must throw them a life preserver to retrieve them from the strong current of sin that pulls them further and further toward destruction.

But as time went along, I discovered something odd, even perplexing. Very few move toward the light or reach for the life preserver. And when we try to convert them, it feels more like pestering the perishing rather than rescuing them. Hardly what we expected from desperate souls!

Seeker Sensitive

As an adult, I joined what is often called a "seeker church," one of those shopping mall–sized campuses with a friendly parking crew, aromatic coffee bar, and cutting-edge worship. Our list of value statements includes phrases like "People matter to God, so they matter to us" and "Excellence honors God and reflects his character" and "Authentic worship is meaningful to believers and seekers alike."

Following the basic principles of marketing, we manage every detail to create a winsome environment and package our message in a manner that people will find attractive (or at least easier to understand). We avoid "Christianese," phrases that might make sense to the "in crowd" but sound foreign to unbelievers. We don't refer to one another as "brother" and "sister," or ask folks to "extend the right hand of fellowship," or sing songs with titles like "Are You Washed in the Blood?" And we never embarrass guests by asking them to stand and identify themselves. In short, we try to make our church a safe place for people to process their spiritual journey or, as our pastor likes to say, "kick the tires of Christianity."

A simple philosophy drives churches like ours: people eager to embrace Christianity are looking for a church sensitive to their needs. And use of progressive language, contemporary music, and comfortable surroundings makes hearing the message and embracing the gospel more likely.

So goes the theory. And on the surface it makes sense—if not for one problem. Hardly any "seekers" are coming. By some estimates, only about 5 percent of those attending churches like mine fit a loosely defined criterion for a seeker. And a case can be made that churches one might call "seeker *in*sensitive" have a similar percentage of converts.

Don't get me wrong. I am not criticizing my church, the seeker movement, or any other earnest attempt to spread the gospel. I'm just not convinced that our approach is any more effective than the hymn-singing, grocery-clerk-confronting style of my childhood congregation. And the reason seems linked to something far more complex than program methodology or presentation style.

America is widely considered a Christian nation, a broad generalization since only about one-third of the population attends religious services with any regularity. But when they do attend, most participate in a Catholic, Protestant, or evangelical church rather than worship in a mosque, temple, or shrine, making us the best approximation of a Christian nation on the planet. So why does a country seen as Christian by the rest of the world have so many people who reject Christianity? If Christ is most evident here, why do so few believe in him?

In fact, despite the "mega-church" phenomenon of the past two decades, American church attendance on the whole hasn't even kept pace with population growth. While we have become more sophisticated in presenting Christ, our population has become less Christian.

Millions who have heard the gospel message have simply said, "No thanks," leaving those of us trying to convince them in a bit of a quandary. Although we lovingly prepare what we believe to be a beautifully garnished meal, they have no interest in eating. And that leaves us with a nagging question: are they honestly not hungry, or are we terrible cooks?

What if those to whom we are throwing out the lifeline don't see themselves as drowning in a sea of despair? What if those for whom we've retooled our churches to be sensitive aren't seeking?

What if they aren't hungry? What if the choice to believe has very little to do with how the message is delivered, and very much to do with how it is received?

But I have an even more troubling question. *What if the choice to believe has less to do with how Christianity is received, and more to do with what is?* Perhaps our message doesn't convince because our message isn't convincing. Or, to use my cooking analogy, maybe we're serving something hard to swallow, something our decorative garnish can't cover.

What Is Christianity?

I should clarify what I mean by "Christianity," since we can't discuss the nature of belief until we understand the object of belief. Some use the word "Christian" as an action verb or code of behavior. To be Christian means being nice to others and living a decent life. Many would find it offensive to be called unchristian, in the same way I might find it offensive to be called uncivilized. Using this definition, the term *Christian* can be applied to any law-abiding citizen who hangs Christmas lights in December.

In this book, I use the word "Christianity" as a noun to refer to a set of beliefs. To be Christian means you embrace the central tenets of the faith: belief in God, sin, the divinity of Christ, and other essential teachings that have defined mainstream Christianity since the start—beliefs summarized by the early church fathers in the Apostles' and Nicene Creeds and used for centuries as the touchstone of orthodoxy by believers of virtually every denomination and persuasion.

As a noun, Christianity means several very specific truths revealed to us by God through the Scriptures and in the person of Jesus Christ. It provides an overarching framework for understanding life and salvation, consistent with the orthodox faith as understood by believers of all times—whether Eastern Orthodox, Roman Catholic, United Presbyterian, or Southern Baptist.

As a noun, Christianity is a worldview sophisticated enough to encompass every academic discipline and resolve life's thorniest problems, while simple enough to prompt a tiny child to sing, "Jesus loves me this I know, for the Bible tells me so."

But why doesn't everyone exposed to it believe it? And what good can come from believers poking into unbelief?

How Fragile?

Two hikes under the ninety-degree heat of a merciless sun behind us, I sit with friends at a picnic table in Mueller State Park, downing a soft drink while discussing my fascination with unbelief. Neither Clark nor Tori have had a crisis of doubt since becoming Christians; both feel confident the doors are locked. They wonder why I think the topic is important.

"Strong faith should not accept easy answers," I reply. "And I worry about our kids." They have five, I have four—most of whom are currently playing in the woods or slapping a mosquito. "A high percentage of those raised in Christianity walk away from it during their first year of college. I believe a big part of the reason is that when confronted with tough questions for the first time, the easy answers they've been given can't win the day."

One can believe something to be true, yet have weak or even faulty reasons for doing so. I believe the microwave heats food; I have no idea why or how. Imagine that I were to encounter an unbelieving professor in the classroom, one who has never used a microwave because he cannot find anyone to make a convincing argument for its utility. If asked to defend my belief, I could easily be made to look and feel foolish. But when I get hungry, I will heat my microwavable, gourmet mac & cheese, while the professor eats a cold, squished PB & J.

While accepting easy answers does not invalidate the object of faith, it can undermine the confidence of faith, especially when confronting hard questions or disenchanting life circumstances.

"My goal is not to argue or try to convince unbelievers," I continue, "but to give them an opportunity to convince me."

They glance at one another before responding. A bit hesitant, Tori asks the question: "But what if they *do* convince you?"—the concern, I suppose, that we all share at one level or another.

How fragile, we wonder, is faith? How difficult or easy would it be to shake our confidence in Christianity? And why would anyone want to open themselves to the possibility? What if the case for unbelief seems more compelling than the case for confidence?

From where I sit today, I can't imagine being convinced by "the other side." I've used the microwave too many times to question its power. My entire being, mind and soul, considers Christianity a framework for life that surpasses all others. I agree with former skeptic C. S. Lewis: "I believe in Christianity as I believe that the Sun has risen, not only because I see it, but because by it I see everything else."[4]

I suppose that someone, somewhere, could shoot a hole in my defense or reveal a flaw in my logic. But my standard for faith is not one hundred percent certainty or watertight evidence for every minor point of Christian theology. Not, "Is Christian belief irrefutable?" but rather, "Is belief more reasonable than unbelief?"

Still, it is high time I stood toe-to-toe with skepticism in order to discover whether and why I might flinch. Until now I've assumed those who reject Christianity do so less because they disagree with its claims than because they dislike its demands. Adopting G. K. Chesterton's view, I've failed to give unbelievers the benefit of the doubt. "The Christian ideal has not been tried and found wanting," he said. "It has been found difficult, and left untried."[5]

I suppose that might be true of many, perhaps most. But it cannot be true of all. There must be those who genuinely disagree with the Christian religion—no axe to grind, no score to settle, no agenda to hide. They understand it, perhaps even respect it.

They just don't buy it.

Not So Simple Faith

Faith is a complicated notion. On one hand, Jesus commended simple, childlike trust:

> Let the little children come to me, and do not hinder them, for the kingdom of heaven belongs to such as these (Matthew 19:14).

> I tell you the truth, anyone who will not receive the kingdom of God like a little child will never enter it (Luke 18:17).

On the other hand, we are told to grow up:

> Therefore let us leave the elementary teachings about Christ and go on to maturity (Hebrews 6:1).

In one place we are told that faith is its own confirmation:

> Now faith is the substance of things hoped for, the evidence of things not seen (Hebrews 11:1 NKJV).

Yet in another place we are directed to build a reasonable case to defend what we believe:

> Always be prepared to give an answer to everyone who asks you to give the reason for the hope that you have (1 Peter 3:15).

So which is it? Childlike simplicity or grown-up maturity? Faith as its own foundation or evidence that demands a verdict?

For me, the answers grow out of understanding the nature of belief itself.

An interesting incident occurred during Jesus' time on earth in which he seemed to lose patience with his followers while demonstrating compassion toward unbelief. A father distressed over his son's convulsive seizures asked, "Teacher, I brought you my son, who is possessed by a spirit that has robbed him of speech. Whenever it seizes him, it throws him to the ground. He foams at the mouth, gnashes his teeth and becomes rigid." Enough for any parent to take whatever steps necessary to relieve his precious boy's suffering! "I asked your disciples to drive out the spirit, but they could not."

So far, nothing out of the ordinary; people asking for help or healing approached Jesus every day. But for some reason, this incident prompted Jesus to express frustration with an unbelief that affected even his closest followers.

"O unbelieving generation," Jesus replied, "how long shall I stay with you? How long shall I put up with you? Bring the boy to me."

Just before healing the boy, Jesus spoke to the father. "Everything is possible for him who believes." In response the father immediately shouted, "I do believe; help me overcome my unbelief!"[6]

What does this story tell us about faith? First, one can believe and doubt something at the same moment. The father believed . . . or at least, thought he believed. Or perhaps wished he believed. All he knew was that he felt desperate to find help for his son, and had enough confidence that Jesus might be able to heal him. Was he certain? No. Did he believe? A little. Did he want to believe even more? Very much so.

Second, strong faith can be incomplete faith. The disciples felt more convinced of Jesus' teachings than anyone. After all, they had left careers, families, stability, even fortunes behind in order to follow a homeless, wandering preacher. But giving up everything to follow him did not equal complete belief or an understanding of everything he said. They may have desired such faith. But they did not possess it.

It seems there is a continuum of belief. Faith is not like a light switch, either on or off, but more like a dimmer knob that can increase or decrease the light, depending upon one's mood.

Ask people whether they believe in God, and you will find most on the far positive end of the continuum. Relatively few in the human race reject the existence of a Supreme Being. But ask how many believe that God is concerned about the details of every life, or whether Jesus is the only way to heaven, and you will find the lights begin to dim.

All of us find ourselves in different places on that continuum, often depending upon the topic at hand. I know some very strong professing Christians who question whether Jesus will return to earth or whether there is a place of eternal damnation called hell. They may not talk about these doubts, but they exist. The dimmer knob moves up and down for all of us, depending upon the statement made.

God is love. A brilliant flash of light.

Jesus died and rose from the grave. An optimistic glimmer.

Jesus is the only way. A faint glow.

God condemns nice people to hell. A barely detectable flicker.

I am convinced that facing Christianity's critics can actually strengthen faith and move us further up the continuum of belief—sort of like facing your greatest fear in order to conquer anxiety. What good comes from timidly hiding under the covers in response to sounds of uncertainty? Checking the locks should not, in my view, undermine faith. It should allow us to crawl back into bed and sleep soundly.

But in order to do so, we must join the distraught father in his prayer. "Lord, I do believe. Now help me overcome my unbelief!" For me, that prayer became intensely real while listening to the unconvinced. A prayer that, in the end, led me to boldly declare, "I still believe!"

Unmet Expectations
—The DISILLUSIONED—

Humpty-Dumpty was pushed!

BUMPER STICKER

CHAPTER 2

Saint Mary Ellen

"I do miss the church."

Mary Ellen sat quietly with the other children on the uncomfortable, rickety wooden folding chairs relegated to the kids. Neither of the congregations in her tiny Appalachian mountain town could afford nice furniture. Grandma attended the "holy roller" church, with lots of shouting, hellfire and brimstone preaching, and speaking in strange, heavenly languages—common in these parts during the early 1950s. But Mary Ellen became frightened attending Sunday school with Grandma, so her parents let her attend the Methodist church, a bit more serious and dignified in its religious expression. Daddy didn't much care. In his opinion, religion would be better off if there were no denominations to cause so much division.

In one of those serious moments in children's church when everyone is asked to bow their heads and close their eyes for prayer and reflection, the minister paused his conversation with God in order to speak directly to the youngsters in a low, somber tone—almost as if the good Lord himself had prompted a time of inward spiritual examination.

"Children, being open and honest before our heavenly Father, I would like to see the hands of everyone who sinned this past week," the minister began. "The Bible tells us if we confess our sins, God is faithful and just to forgive us our sins. But we must begin with the recognition of our need. So let me see your hands if you know you did something wrong since last Sunday."

During the few moments allotted for reflection, Mary Ellen dutifully rehearsed the past seven days in her mind. At ten-and-a-half-years old, opportunities for serious mischief come few and far between. She thought of that moment in gym class when the teacher introduced a form of gymnastics that looked and felt a whole lot like dancing, a Methodist no-no. But Mary Ellen did more awkward stumbling than graceful floating, so that wouldn't make the cut.

On a few occasions she resented being asked to do her chores, but she had checked her attitude so quickly that she doubted whether Mom or Dad took notice. So she scratched those episodes off her mental checklist. She had played no cards, uttered no bad words, thrown no temper tantrums. Mary Ellen had pretty much remained on the straight and narrow all week long. So she kept her hands folded in her lap.

Meanwhile, every other kid had lifted his or her hand (whether from a sense of profound conviction or a desire to satisfy the minister's expectations, remained unclear). Either way, it left Mary Ellen in the unenviable position of being the only self-righteous child in class.

"Mary Ellen!" came the stern, disapproving voice of the minister. "Raise your hand!"

She never forgot that moment. Five decades later she still describes it as embarrassing and confusing. Innocent of the crime, she was ordered to confess her guilt.

The incident symbolizes the disillusionment Mary Ellen has encountered time after time in her attempts to fit into Christianity. She has tried to understand and embrace a faith in which she has never felt entirely at home.

"I would describe myself as a good person," she says. "I had to find a place in the world for myself that is not that strict and not that judgmental."

Now about sixty years old, Mary Ellen radiates an insecure beauty and warmth that well suits her work with geriatric and brain-injured patients. Her disheveled, mostly blonde hair and echo of a once lovely figure suggest a woman who, when younger, may have turned heads while fulfilling her maternal responsibilities, raising Kevin and Sharon. Surprisingly articulate, considering that she grew up in a Smoky Mountain town of five hundred, Mary Ellen overcame more obstacles and baggage than most to achieve an impressive academic and professional standing.

Mary Ellen works as a counselor. She exudes kindness and compassion, the kind of person anyone would gladly call "friend" or "confidant." Clearly a good listener, she feels a bit awkward being interviewed—more accustomed to hearing from others than taking center stage. But Mary Ellen agreed to help me with the research for my book as one more way she could help others, allowing them to learn from the ups and downs of her own journey.

A journey that includes the painful realities of a broken world.

Broken

For twenty-five years Mary Ellen was married to Frank, a man she calls "the most closed person I have ever met." His tough exterior and solitary personality dovetailed with his military career. But it didn't promote intimacy. Eventually the marriage became too difficult for a very open, nurturing woman like Mary Ellen. "We lived in silence with one another for years," she remembers. "And after a while, silence does horrible things to you."

And so, after two and a half quiet decades, Mary Ellen did the most difficult thing she has ever done: she filed for divorce. Since the kids had grown, she saw no reason to continue the façade.

The separation proved amicable and the two became pretty good friends. He served as her handyman when something broke around the house, and she reminded him to eat right—

almost as if they had been lifelong friends who had never married. They lived apart for decades until, in 1999, doctors discovered Frank had a terminal brain tumor. And so, consistent with her compassionate, maternal nature, Mary Ellen took Frank into her home and nursed him through the seven-month ordeal of surgery, radiation, and chemotherapy. No wonder Sharon, Mary Ellen's daughter, calls her mother, "Saint Mary Ellen of Cumberland Gap."

"I'm no saint," responds an embarrassed Mary Ellen. Perhaps not. But she certainly has more of the stuff saints are made of than most of us.

Mary Ellen brought the kids to the Methodist church until her divorce, at which point she gave up trying to practice the faith she had known since childhood. For a while, she sampled a variety of churches, everything from Catholic mass to energetic African American churches—a big step for someone raised in the culture of segregation. She learned to love the tranquility of liturgy and the inspiration of black gospel music. But nothing ever felt quite comfortable.

I thought of the many boring sermons I had endured while sitting on hard, wooden pews, and wondered whether anyone feels entirely comfortable in church. But something deeper than sore bottoms caused by long-winded preachers bothered Mary Ellen.

"Why?" I ask. "Was there a specific reason, or did you just lose interest?"

"I guess I just felt out of place, maybe because church seems more suited to families—there is a stigma associated with being a divorced, single woman." Whether that stigma is real or perceived, Mary Ellen can't say. "I do miss church. I still see myself as Christian. But I worship differently, finding a walk in nature more spiritual than attending church."

Mary Ellen, like several I've met during interviews, feels out of place in church. Like me, she grew up regularly attending. Like me, she once quoted Bible verses and sang Jesus choruses on a weekly basis. Like me, she felt it important to bring her young children to church.

Unlike me, something caused her to abandon the whole thing.

Reasonable Expectations

Did Mary Ellen expect too much from the church? I don't think so.

I ask Mary Ellen to summarize her understanding of essential Christian beliefs. Rather than recite a creed, she offers an expectation. "Christianity is about treating your fellow man with respect and dignity. I wouldn't explain it as beliefs such as the Trinity, but how we live our lives and treat other people. But I've seen man's inhumanity to man, including those who call themselves Christians."

What troubles Mary Ellen most about Christianity?

"I am a very nonjudgmental person. It bothers me when Christians see everything so black and white without considering individual situations."

She cites several examples of people who have experienced some type of rejection, including a friend who was asked not to attend a church-sponsored Bible study after her brother died of AIDS.

"I resent that gays are not welcome within a lot of churches. It reminds me of the anger I felt as a child in the South when my black friend was not allowed to go certain places with me."

On one level, I must agree with Mary Ellen. The church should play a redemptive role in our world, helping to heal the broken, rescue the perishing, love the outcast. I would call her expectations reasonable. And I relate to her outrage when Christians behave in an unloving manner. The largest Baptist church in my segregated suburban Detroit neighborhood refused to baptize African Americans because it didn't allow black members. An effeminate boy in my junior high school was teased and labeled "fag" by other church-going kids. Both make me angry because they run counter to the love of Christ we proclaim.

But I have learned to accept the unfortunate reality that idiots reside in every group, including the church. The downside of grace is that it invites all comers, jerks or not. Wondering why Mary Ellen hasn't taken a similarly pragmatic view, I quickly discover that her concern runs much deeper.

A Nice God

"I can't believe in a God who is a punishing God," she declares. It bothers Mary Ellen that Christians call homosexuality sin. "This isn't a lifestyle that someone would choose. I have several good friends who are lesbian." Her voice becomes hushed at this point to a near whisper. "And almost all of them have experienced some type of sexual abuse."

Once again, Mary Ellen's compassionate heart and concern for hurting people surfaces. She has spent a lifetime accepting those most try to avoid; she has sacrificed herself in order to care for folks most consider damaged goods. Why, she wonders, doesn't the church do the same? She had enough Bible teaching to know that Jesus said Christians should be identified by the love they show for one another. From Mary Ellen's perspective, we must be a disappointment.

I suppose that, given the opportunity, most of us would try to make God in our own image. A God in the image of Mary Ellen would be a very nice God—one who loves everyone, forgives everything, judges nothing.

I read Mary Ellen a passage from the popular book *Conversations with God* and ask for her reaction to the author's view of the Almighty.

> Evil is that which you call evil. Yet even that I love ... I do not love hot more than cold, high more than low, left more than

right. It is all relative. It is all part of what is ... I do not love "good" more than I love "bad." Hitler went to heaven. When you understand this, you will understand God.[1]

A long silence hangs in the air as Mary Ellen ponders the idea of Hitler going to heaven. She doesn't want to believe in a God who punishes. But a man who devised the Holocaust should pay. How does one reconcile the desire that God loves all with the need for him to judge some?

"I don't have an answer to that," comes her honest reply.

"Do you believe in a good God?" I ask, hoping to discover the root of Mary Ellen's hesitancy.

"Yes, I do believe God is good." An effortless reply.

"Do you believe he punishes evil?"

Again, a long silence. I can see in her eyes the wrestling match taking place within. Like the rest of us, she feels intense anger over a man sexually abusing the innocent child, or the ruthless leader exterminating Jews and other sacred lives. She wants them punished. But by whom? The God she worships while walking in nature loves and accepts; he does not judge and condemn. My Christian theology says he is both. But Mary Ellen left that view of our heavenly Father behind in favor of one reluctant to scold while eager to console.

"I don't have an answer for that either." A hung jury.

Disillusioned

So where does all of this leave Mary Ellen, the once-faithful Methodist who now feels out of place among traditional Christians? Would she describe herself as a Christian who has stopped going to church, or as a person who has moved away from particularly Christian beliefs?

"My beliefs are not so structured that I'm open only to Christianity," she replies. Clearly, she would wince at Jesus' claim to be the only way. "I wonder why the church is necessary for spirituality. I am not interested in dogma, even though I miss the context and even the ritual of formal religion."

I grew up in a church culture that condemned playing cards, dancing, going to movies, even reading from modern Bible translations. It wasn't easy untangling the culturally-influenced standards of a particular religious environment from larger questions of morality. But eventually I learned to see a world of difference between minor cultural taboos and clear biblical mandates, such as avoiding adultery and homosexuality. And while I feel for those who find themselves wrestling with desires condemned by the church—I am well aware of the unbearable self-loathing such a conflict ignites—I accept what the Bible teaches.

Many, like Mary Ellen, react against the whole system, lumping the big and small prohibitions together and seeking solace in a God too nice to care. The problem, of course, is that such a reaction creates a different, bigger problem. It causes one to feel out of place with a religion based upon the objective, sometimes hard realities of right and wrong, good and evil, love and justice. And it forces people like Mary Ellen into the lingering quagmire of disillusionment.

I wish Mary Ellen still embraced Christianity. She is the kind of person who could be part of the solution for the church, rather than part of the problem. Her loving heart and willing self-sacrifice would help us reflect a much better image of Christlike compassion. In fact, I think she retains the residual fabric of Christian belief. That is why Mary Ellen wishes the church were more loving and becomes angry when some Christians display a critical spirit and fail to fulfill a redemptive role in the lives of others.

Mary Ellen began her story recalling an unpleasant moment when a minister singled her out for failing to raise her hand along with the other kids. I suspect she never entirely outgrew her childhood experience, sitting in church among strict, judgmental believers. Today, like then, she considers herself a good person, unable to recall any particular sins committed amid her lifelong efforts to love the unlovable, help the needy, and comfort the hurting.

In fact, some even call her a saint.

Hard To Swallow

Christianity calls "good" people sinners.

CHAPTER 3

Fallen Angel

"If I had lived in Jesus' time, knowing what I know today,
I probably would have said,
'There's a medication for that delusion.'"

Jonathan wants to be a good Christian. He'd like to believe with his whole heart, mind, and body. But the latter keeps dragging him back into a miserable pit of despair, a crater from which only God could rescue him—something the Almighty seems unwilling to do, despite repeated requests.

In his late forties, Jonathan is handsomely haggard, the apparent victim of his own bad habits. I see a resignation in his eyes, like a fallen angel cut off from redemption. He seems weary from decades of trying to claw his way back to a wholesome joy, always just out of reach.

"I have more faith than ever in my life," Jonathan explains when I ask about his present spiritual status. "I have a deep desire to know God, a feeling that he is the air that I breathe. Because of that, I'm more aware of how difficult it is for me to put faith into practice—following moral laws, living in harmony with God, things like that."

Jonathan describes a gap in his life. On one side sits a scale labeled "Desire for God." Here things look good, the dimmer knob is turned up pretty high. On the other side sits a scale measuring "Obedience to God"—and that one tells a far different tale.

"Right now I'm doing things that would probably discount me as a good Christian," he says. His open confession of failure seems refreshingly honest, but also kind of sad. "I am doing them because they dull the pain."

The pain, I would soon discover, runs very deep—rooted in another of Jonathan's honest, sad confessions. "I guess I know God is there, but I still doubt that he's enough."

To better understand his pain and doubt, we rewind the tape to a third-grade Johnny, attending a Catholic grade school, thanks to a scholarship. His mother, divorced from an alcoholic husband, could never afford the tuition; she barely makes ends meet for her six kids, despite hard work and frugal living. So, out of respect for his grandmother's long-term membership and support, the church-run school waives all expenses.

Jonathan has strong memories of those days, perhaps the happiest of his life: early morning catechism classes; the sense of comfort and belonging that come from the discipline and order of a well-defined belief system; the beauty and tranquility experienced through choral music, prayers, and liturgy. As an altar boy, little Johnny numbered himself among the most devoted of Catholic kids you could ever meet; he hoped one day to become a priest.

"I had many magical moments in church where I knew God was with me," Jonathan recalls. "Like when I was the only boy soprano in the choir, singing those wonderful high notes that seemed to touch the very soul of God. I loved it! I remember praying as a small child, knowing with all my heart that God was right there with me."

Maybe he was. But things changed, making it feel as if Johnny's cozy, intimate God began inching farther and farther away.

The letter from the church to Johnny's mom, requesting that she tithe, lest they withdraw his scholarship.

Her indignant response, pulling him from the school he loved.

Moving to public school in fourth grade, where spiritual entropy began to drain his zeal for God.

There had never been any faith reinforcement at home, so losing his connection with spirituality at school fed a dwindling connection to Christianity. Like any relationship, Jonathan's passion died due to inattentiveness.

And so the church that once represented safety and belonging gradually became suspect and irrelevant. Jonathan attended less frequently, eventually matching his mother's semi-annual appearance for key holidays like Easter and Christmas.

"It just got too hard," Jonathan reflects. He describes the joy of playing in the very first guitar mass at his church, newly approved after Vatican II, in an effort to use his exceptional musical gifts in service to God. "But I felt all on my own because my mom wasn't supportive or around. I recall riding my bike to mass practice, trying to steer while carrying my guitar without a case."

My heart aches for Jonathan as I sense the abandonment he must have felt, trying to be a good little Christian all on his own.

"Experiences like that represented an ill-fated attempt to continue a relationship with the church," he says. "Nobody ever helped me integrate Christianity into a lifestyle. So, either from disuse or neglect, Christianity slowly dissipated from my life.

"My parents were divorced, which carried quite a stigma. I was the son of a sinner, with no redemptive options. A cardinal sin, divorce is something you could confess but not escape. So I felt like an orphan or refugee of the faith."

The lingering, unspoken condemnation became too much.

"I rejected the church entirely after confirmation," Jonathan recalls. "In fact, my eyes are red and puffy in my confirmation photograph because I had been fighting with my mother. She insisted that I go through confirmation, I think for my grandmother's sake, and I didn't want to go. By that time I had come to view the whole thing as a sham."

Fallen

"I'd almost say that my thoughts about God from age twelve to seventeen were virtually non-existent, as if the day of my confirmation was the day I decided to stop worshiping God," Jonathan says as he begins to describe his fall from grace. "The secular world I was starting to enjoy gradually crept in and forced out any hope of a religious world."

The passion for music in this former choirboy soprano and mass guitarist needed a new outlet. So at fifteen, Jonathan got together with several other talented kids and launched a rock band. Better than their years, they landed one paying gig after another. It all suggested a bright future. So bright, in fact, that a former Methodist youth minister—a very charismatic, driven guy who seemed capable of moving them to the next level—agreed to become their manager. He lined up auditions and generated pretty good income for the kids.

"It was fantastic!" Jonathan recalls.

But as the story often goes, the manager turned out to be a sexual predator, hoping to take more from Jonathan and his starstruck partners than they were willing to give. His advances failed, but added another betrayal to Jonathan's ledger sheet. "We were lonely kids trusting a guy who had been a church minister," he says. Not surprisingly, the band Jonathan loved and dreamed of riding into infamy dispersed.

Thanks a lot, God!

Months later, yet another defining moment occurred. Jonathan's mom decided to move the family a thousand miles north. Nearly an adult, seventeen-year-old Jonathan took his opportunity to bolt the nest by remaining in Los Angeles. And so, the last shaky vestige of constancy slipped out of Jonathan's life.

"At seventeen, I lived alone in Los Angeles," Jonathan continues. "I landed a job with a commune-like health food store. All of the employees were invited to eat whatever they wanted from the store and restaurant—one big, happy family. The four owners were followers of the same eastern religion guru—very mystical spiritualism including yoga, animism, and a variety of new age practices."

And how did all of this impact an impressionable, disillusioned Catholic boy?

"I felt afloat," Jonathan recalls. "I knew there was a God, but at this point became infused with the idea that there is no one place to find him; at least no reliable place to find him."

He began practicing an intense form of yoga.

"I had this vague idea that if I did the right things I could generate that feeling I had when I was six and sitting in church. But I didn't associate the feeling of spiritual belonging with what I had been taught in church. I associated it with the experience of pure awe I had sitting in the pews during morning mass—wonderful moments of transcendence and reverence."

As if spiritually orphaned, seventeen-year-old Johnny was trying hard to get back home. But he had given up hope of finding it through traditional Christianity.

Jonathan's experience reminds me of an experiment conducted with fish in a tank. Repeatedly banging their noses against a clear sheet of glass at feeding time, they could not reach the food just beyond. So they became conditioned to consider eating impossible. Later, after the glass was removed, the fish starved to death because they ignored food particles floating right in front of their eyes.

A hungry Jonathan, like those fish, had hit the glass once too often.

"So I turned to the idea of finding God within," he explains. New age theology is about looking inside for truth, rather than submitting to divine revelation. "That gave me some relief, although it did feel mechanical—as if by repeating the right mantra I would become enlightened. But I was ambitious, so I dove in and tried it all—much like I did in church."

"Did you study the beliefs or just engage in the practices?" I ask, hoping to uncover whether the young Johnny fish became a naïve victim.

"I read books on Tibetan Buddhism and the basic tenets of Sikhism," he explains. "And I familiarized myself with reincarnation, karma, purifying the soul, enlightenment, and the rest. I became highly focused on finding God through metaphysical techniques, including a full year of psychic training. I immersed myself in the spiritual world, even spending several years earning my living through spiritual readings."

So much for the naïve victim.

"It was all very egocentric," Jonathan shivers, a menacing stare betraying the memory of dark realities encountered during his quest for enlightenment. Even after one has escaped the demonic practice of channeling, a dreadful echo remains. "I totally lost touch with the idea that there was anything above me. God was what I saw in the spirit world through various practices and rituals."

For more than a decade, Jonathan lived in a world frighteningly foreign to most Christians, a world in which unwholesome spiritual realities eclipsed the light of God he had loved and lost.

"I would like to have hung out in the traditional church. But they didn't offer me a thing," he says, both regret and resentment punctuating his words, as if he's trying to decide whether to blame himself or unspecified others. "The whole gambit of traditional resources had let me down. I lost any connection to the possibility that God was relevant to my daily life. So I tried to find it through metaphysics."

It didn't work. And his nose bounced off yet another plate of glass.

Full Circle?

Jonathan plans to attend a Christian twelve-step meeting this evening after our interview, summarizing the dichotomous reality of his post-cult life. For more than fifteen years, he has followed in his alcoholic father's footsteps, slipping in and out of drunken binges, treatment facilities, and life on the streets. During his up times, he writes and sings music, including an occasional demo sent to Nashville. A quick listen to some of Jonathan's songs reveals real talent—all the more reason for him to feel cheated whenever life deals him another blow.

More often than not, Jonathan's binges of sobriety occur thanks to the support and charity of Christians, be they rescue mission volunteers or fellow recovering addicts. He has never gone back to the Catholic church of his childhood, but he has wandered in and out of several protestant, evangelical, and charismatic congregations. Most have featured well-meaning, if unsophisticated folks, who provide him a much-needed point of connection to a wavering faith.

As I run through my final interview questions, Jonathan's answers suggest his efforts to reconnect with Christianity have had some affect.

What are the basic teachings of Christianity?

"Man is sinful, unable to get it right on his own," he begins. "There is one God, the Creator, whose core nature is love. And because that God knew that we could not redeem ourselves, he sent his Son to not only demonstrate how we should live, but also take on the responsibility for our spiritual growth by dying and rising again."

A good start! But as Jonathan continues, it becomes increasingly clear that he has yet to abandon unorthodox teachings absorbed during his metaphysical journey.

"Through his dying and rising, we have the opportunity to go beyond our status as human beings. We are not lost anymore because we can be in touch with the divine through the divine having become human." I sense his struggle as he tries to meld two very different views of Jesus into a single answer. "We can have a relationship with God and that relationship can be fostered through Jesus Christ."

How is Christianity different from and similar to other religions?

"One of the main differences is that you are not relating to a human being who says he knows about God, but with a person who was God in human form. The similarities include a moral code, going beyond yourself to become a better person, joining with others in a religious experience."

What do you find odd or offensive about Christianity?

"The judgmental attitude that seems to come from people in organized religion that seems to be opposite of what Christ taught—using it as a way to push people away rather than become closer to them."

Is there anything that Christ specifically taught that you find troubling?

"When he said that the only way you can get to the Father is through him." The source of Jonathan's earlier internal conflict becomes clear. "I mean, if a cult leader like David Koresh had said that, some of his followers would have believed him. But most of us would say he was crazy. If I had lived in Jesus' time, knowing what I know today, I probably would have said, 'There's a medication for that delusion.'"

Next, I ask Jonathan to react to statements associated with traditional Christian teachings.

We are sinners.

"No doubt about it. We are hardwired for self-destruction." Jonathan's own life patterns have reinforced this notion beyond question. "But I used to struggle with that concept, especially during the era of my life when I wanted to believe that higher consciousness could bring about the needed changes in my life."

Unbelievers go to hell.

"I have a hard time with that one. The idealist in me wants to believe some redemptive power is going to reach everybody, sooner or later. I know that's not what the Bible says. It makes me sad to think about." Jonathan comments on his mother who has clearly rejected belief in Jesus Christ. "I don't want to say for sure, and I don't want to imagine it. To be honest, it seems kind of cruel. It is frankly one of the most uncomfortable parts of Christianity for me."

Jesus claimed to be the only way to heaven.

"I believe he said that, and I think he meant it. I believe it for me; I am pointing myself in that direction. But I don't want to believe it for others." Several long pauses and hesitant comments suggest Jonathan is most uncomfortable trying to resolve this one. He clearly wants to believe Jesus is God in the flesh, but has not entirely abandoned the generic spirituality adopted while immersed in eastern pantheism. In that world, Jesus is one among many, a notion in direct opposition to what Jesus claimed about himself.

"I have decided that Jesus is the only way for me," Jonathan continues, "which is a very big step, to be honest with you. I used to be a pseudo-intellectual guy who believed there are many forms of God and it doesn't matter since the spirit will find its way as long as you are sincere. To decide there is only one way for me in Jesus Christ is a big step, and I have a hard time saying it has to be true for everyone else."

I ask Jonathan what he thinks drives him toward belief, no matter how faint, while others seem entirely disinterested. What makes someone like him long for God when so many couldn't care less?

"I think it comes down to experience. Some people, for example, have lives that are for the most part under control. I think they tend to question or doubt God. Others, like me, have confronted the hard reality of how weak and vulnerable we really are. When you find yourself flat on your back on the cold, snowy streets, you have no choice but to cry out to God!"

As we conclude our conversation, Jonathan summarizes his experience and why, despite a deep desire for God, he hesitates to enter the fray of traditional Christianity.

"I don't want to meet another unchristian Christian. Whether due to my Catholic background, the hurt caused by that Methodist youth minister, or whatever, I have a basic distrust of the church. I feel safer getting on my knees in my apartment and developing my own life with Christ than allowing it to be stepped on by others. But at least I haven't said, 'Because the church hurt me, God doesn't exist.'" In his case, I guess that's quite an accomplishment.

Jonathan still clearly feels disillusioned—whether with himself or with God is difficult to say. Either way, he represents countless others who find the Christian way hard to follow ... and to swallow.

Hard To Swallow

Christianity is too hard.

Aimless Wandering

—The SEEKER—

Believe those who seek the truth.
Doubt those who find it.

BUMPER STICKER

CHAPTER 4

Dabblers

"I would personally like to think that the Muslim God,
the Hindu God, the Buddhist God,
and the Christian God are the same God."

An assortment of appetizers and desserts crowd the kitchen table, small paper plates balancing on the edge next to a bowl of tortilla chips and some specially prepared Mexican bean dip. Wishing I had skipped dinner, I dutifully fill my plate and enter the adjoining living room with the others. The setting looks and feels like a typical small group Bible study: a handful of friendly people enjoying high-fat foods and soda while seated in a circle on a long couch and folding chairs. As the only outsider, I can tell the seven regulars feel quite chummy with one another, thanks to years of participation in what organizers label a "Food for Thought" gathering.

I will be interviewing the group, a collection of independent thinkers from various cultural, political, and religious backgrounds who meet monthly to discuss the latest controversy. Earlier topics have included homosexual rights, the place of religion in the public square, and differing opinions on life after death. The city launched these "Food for Thought" clusters in an effort to foster respect and unity in an otherwise divided town. They figured if those who disagree met to chat over soda and Mexican bean dip every now and then, civility might prevail whenever the city council faced its next polarizing debate. Whether the strategy worked doesn't seem to matter to the seven folks gathered on this evening. They just enjoy one another's diverse company.

And I do mean diverse, something that becomes apparent after asking each person to briefly describe his or her current religious status: two evangelical Christians; one recovering Catholic; and four who could be called "dabblers."

I got the label from Neil when he described his own religious history: "I'm not an atheist. I was raised Catholic. I don't go to church or practice any particular religion. I don't know how to define myself. I dabble, I guess." In his late thirties, stocky build with a mild demeanor, Neil looks a bit like the kid in high school everyone liked but who ate lunch alone anyway. Despite regular participation in mass and catechism during childhood, Christianity didn't take. "When I turned fourteen, my parents gave me a choice, so I left the church. I didn't buy into it, feeling it was just a story. I'm sure there was a bit of kid rebellion mixed in, but the whole thing seemed weird to me—so I rejected it all."

I ask Neil to describe his "dabbling" in more detail. "I visit the Congregational church downtown once in a while, whenever I hit a rough spot in my life." He explained further, "I've tried a variety of churches, but for some reason I am turned off by those that seem casual and unorganized." He recalls a few incidents visiting Charismatic services. "Maybe it is a carryover from my Catholic upbringing, but I think to myself, *This isn't a church. This is a 7-Eleven with a clown. They're nuts!*" I guess Neil feels more comfortable with the sane church he rejected.

Could Neil summarize the basic beliefs of Christianity? He takes a stab. "I think it is just belief in Jesus Christ and his teachings. I don't know all of what goes into that, but he is at the center."

Next to Neil sits Donna, who describes herself as "An unaffiliated, sort-of Christian. Whatever that means." Her tense laughter suggests embarrassment, perhaps worried such a vague description seems unrefined. I get the impression that Donna, a fifty-something wife and mother, enjoys hanging around sophisticated people who prop up her hesitant confidence. "I believe in God, Jesus, and the Bible as a source of truth, but not as the final source. When I do attend church, which isn't often, I go to the Unitarian Church. A fringe Christian might be a good description."

I suppose you could call Donna a second generation "fringe believer" since her father, raised Catholic, married her German Lutheran mother. Rather than choose between the two denominations, they "did a little bit of nothing" with the kids, making hers a non-religious upbringing. Donna married a man who grew up in and was turned off by the Baptist church, so they followed in her parents' footsteps and did nothing religious with their children beyond Christmas and Easter church visits. "We did teach them the golden rule and the existence of a higher being," she quickly and defensively adds.

"I believe I have a great deal of spirituality," she continues. "But to me it does not require church on an every-Sunday basis to have a good relationship with God."

"You're a lapsed dabbler?" someone asks with a laugh. The rest of the group chuckles at the label. And since she figures they are laughing with her rather than at her, Donna joins in with a big smile.

As with Neil, I ask Donna for a summary of the basics of Christian belief. "As I understand it," she strains, "Jesus Christ is the Son of God, sent to earth to teach us how to live and how to die. He died and was resurrected so that we could all have life everlasting."

Pretty good for a lapsed dabbler.

Moving around the room, we come next to Wade, a fiftyish guy with black hair and dark complexion suggesting an unidentifiably mixed racial heritage, possibly including Native American. I have a hard time following Wade, in part because he mumbles softly, forcing me to strain and repeat my requests in order to catch what he says; but also because he seems intent on avoiding any sort of label or pre-defined box for his religious orientation. He doesn't like me asking about his current religious status.

"Are you talking religious or spiritual?" I've always disliked it when people force that distinction, such as when believers say things like "I am talking about relationship, not religion." I understand and agree with their point. But the separation feels unnecessarily forced.

"Both or either," I respond, avoiding his trap.

"I believe I am progressing, and I've always been a spiritually sensitive person," Wade begins. I wonder whether by "spiritually sensitive" he means a sensitive heart or something more like a sensitive tooth; does his story hide deep pain? "I am a searcher and a seeker of the truth. I receive spirituality in many ways. I believe that all religions have a piece of the truth, and that all deviate a little bit."

Moving from the present to childhood, I learn that Wade has indeed experienced the sensitive tooth of religious abuse. His family was deeply entrenched in the Worldwide Church of God, a highly control-oriented cult led by Herbert W. Armstrong, the man I vaguely recall repeatedly setting and missing the date of Jesus' return during the 1970s. I've met others from that movement and I see the same look in Wade's eyes—like a cowering, abused puppy who would get defiant if he weren't so afraid of the next slap.

"It is a difficult thing to leave a cult," Wade continues. "Most people have no idea . . ." His voice trails off, as if the unpleasant memories make it impossible for him to continue this line of thought. He hits fast-forward, moving to the next significant scene in his spiritual journey. "During my late teens, after leaving the Worldwide Church, I got into meditation—and I am still searching and seeking. Because of those early experiences, I am not open to the structure of religion."

As I piece together bits of mumbled phrases, Wade's experience begins to take shape. After leaving his parents' cult, he spent three decades avoiding formal religion. (When you have been burned in the bonfire of religious abuse, I suppose even a candle can make you nervous.) He gravitated toward mystical, quasi-pantheistic spirituality, mixed with skepticism. Wade took pride in his tendency to question the motives of anyone considered a religious leader. "What I love is what we are doing now," he smiles, "sitting around, informally discussing spiritual matters. I love the genuine. I love the sincere. It's got to be the real thing."

Asked for his summary of basic Christianity, Wade becomes clearly uncomfortable, reminding me that he dislikes boxes. "The definition of Christianity is complete love," he reluctantly offers. "It is to have the entire God living in you."

I try pinning Wade down to something more precise, but to no avail. He seems content with his inability to clearly explain, somehow taking comfort in ambiguity and the eternal "searching and seeking" it allows.

At last I come to Sarah, our host for the evening. A glance at the wall decorations and bookshelf selections suggests that Sarah favors a sort of eastern religion, perhaps Hindu or Buddhist. Her physical appearance reinforces the notion: with a very slight frame and attire echoing a 1960s flower child.

"I guess, like Neil, I'd call myself a dabbler," Sarah begins. "I don't really believe in God, but I believe in the idea of God. And I can see why people believe because it would be nice to have, but I don't."

I feel surprised that one who believes only in the idea rather than the reality of God surrounds herself with so many religiously oriented paintings and books. The rest of her story helps fill in the blanks. Raised a very staid and stoic Episcopalian, Sarah retains a level of respect for her parents' beliefs.

"Both of my parents are people who I think of as truly religious, in that what they do and how they treat other people has a religious basis. One of the reasons I have some good feelings about Christianity is I see how generous and kind and thoughtful my parents are."

Sarah loves the church her folks currently attend because, unlike so many others, "it welcomes anyone and everyone"—the denomination's code language for accepting gay priests and couples.

"If there is such a thing as being a true Christian, I'd say my parents are," she continues. "But I think that other religions embody that same idea of treating others the way you'd like to be treated yourself."

Out of the corner of my eye I catch Donna nodding in recognition of the "golden rule" she taught her kids.

"I've also had some influence from eastern religions that have been really positive," she explains. After college, Sarah went to Nepal with the Peace Corps, where she lived within and among Hindu and Buddhist cultures. She never formally studied the teachings of either, but found herself impressed by belief systems that felt less rigid and structured, more organic to daily life.

"I enjoyed the experience of living among those for whom these belief systems were simply part of the fabric of their society, and that many were Hindu and Buddhist at the same time without seeing a conflict," she explains. Sarah considers the Dali Lama her hero because he seems to live a peaceful lifestyle. And yet, she never formally became Buddhist.

She also admires one of my heroes, C. S. Lewis. She has read quite a bit of his writings. Maybe that is part of the reason Sarah retains a residue of goodwill for Christianity. "I'm really conflicted," she says. "In many ways, I have somewhat a positive feeling toward Christianity. I light candles for friends who have died. I love the ritual and ceremony associated with religion. There have been times in my life when I have prayed and hoped that it went somewhere."

Curious about what might have pushed Sarah away from the faith for which she retains so much goodwill, I uncover the usual suspect: a college philosophy class that, in her words, "made me think a lot about belief, existentialism, atheism, Christianity, history, and how they are all interrelated." In other words, she had a biased professor, evidenced by her recap of history as a series of atrocities carried out in the name of religions like Christianity.

"I know it sounds naïve to say so," Sarah admits, "but it is hard for me to understand how people who believe in God could do such things."

How does Sarah define Christianity? A long pause suggesting serious contemplation precedes a reference to something a believing cousin shared with her.

"He said that Christianity is the only religion that has complete forgiveness as one of its main tenets"—a good summary, but one Sarah doesn't buy. "I'm not sure I agree with that, but it is one of the things that people say defines Christianity." Almost as an afterthought, she adds a few more defining tenets. "There is also the Holy Trinity of Father, Son, and Holy Ghost, that somehow the three entities are one-in-the-same in sort of an odd way. There is life after death, which is not only in Christianity but is, I think, an important part of it."

"Anything specific about Jesus?" I ask.

"Yes, that he actually died for our sins and then came back to life."

Clearly, some of her church lessons stuck. So, where did such an eclectic history leave Sarah?

"I would personally like to think that the Muslim God, the Hindu God, the Buddhist God, and the Christian God are the same God."

"Is that what you would like to think, or what you do think?" I prod.

"Well, as I said, I don't really believe in God. But I think the God that people create spiritually, if there is one, is the same."

⌒

I pose one final question to the group. "How do you explain the fact that others fully embrace Christian belief, while you don't? I have spoken to folks who believe, who have stories and experiences remarkably similar to those you've shared tonight. Why do you think they accept what you reject?"

"The Lord works in mysterious ways," Donna takes a stab. "God exists in all of us, pursues all of us differently, asks us all to follow him differently because we all have different paths to pursue. Some people have questioning to do in different ways. We all have our works to do, and God has set up differently how he has us do them. Some choose to be born again Christians to know God. Others choose to know God in other ways." According to Donna, who believes in many ways to God, it is his plan for us to choose divergent paths.

Sarah hesitantly offers a different viewpoint.

"I think in some ways it is easier to believe than not believe," she says. "I would really like to believe because I think it would be comforting." In other words, those who believe, do so for the same reason my daughter sleeps with her teddy bear: it just feels better.

Finally, Neil haltingly offers an explanation that he admits could make him sound like a jerk. "What makes me different from those who believe is that they are able to suspend some of their questions, or suspend reality and just say they believe by faith. But I feel like I just can't stop asking questions, and the answers I get just don't satisfy. I don't think I'm smarter or anything like that. It's just that I feel there are a lot of questions that aren't answered, and maybe someone who believes can just take it on faith."

"What a jerk!" someone jokingly jibes. But I appreciate his honesty. His questions haven't been answered to his satisfaction, making it difficult for him to take the faith leap. Of course, as you might expect from the lead dabbler, he doesn't seem serious about pursuing those answers.

As I finish my list of questions, I glance down and notice that I have taken only one bite of each selection scooped onto my plate. I had spent the evening merely playing with my food to keep up appearances. I consider myself in good company: a group of dabblers spending their lives nibbling around the edges of spirituality without ever really digging in.

Smorgasbord

My visit with the "Food for Thought" group reminds me of a *Life* magazine cover story from several years earlier in which a photo-laced essay summarized the many views of God found in some of the major and minor religious movements of America. From solemn women in a Salt Lake City Tabernacle, to prostrate men facing Mecca as they pray, to smiling singers at a Billy Graham crusade, the author shows and describes some of the largest faith groups of our culture—including Catholics, Protestants, Evangelicals, Mormons, and Jews. He also highlights less visible but growing sects such as Hindus, Buddhists, and Holy Rollers, as well as Greek and Russian Orthodox believers.

The feature writer was Frank McCourt, a lapsed Catholic who became the wildly successful author of the book *Angela's Ashes*. His final paragraph summarized well the perspective of many in this generation: "I don't confine myself to the faith of my fathers anymore. All the religions are spread before me, a great spiritual smorgasbord, and I'll help myself, thank you."[1]

Like all dabblers, McCourt will pick and choose the portions of various faiths that he likes, leaving behind those he doesn't.

Jeremiah Creedon seconds the motion. He wrote a story titled *Designer God* for a leading alternative media magazine in which he posed the telling question, "In a mix-and-match world, why not create your own religion?" Creedon suggests we embrace what has been labeled "cafeteria religion" as a new approach to faith and the truest spiritual quest of all. The opening paragraph says it all.

> A friend of mine I'll call Anne-Marie is the founder of a new religious faith. Like other belief systems throughout the ages, the sect of Anne-Marie exists to address life's most haunting questions. If I ask her why we're born and what happens when we die, her answers suggest that our time on earth has meaning and purpose. Whether I buy it hardly matters. The sect of Anne-Marie has one member, Anne-Marie, and that's plenty.[2]

The "mix-and-match" approach to faith has its own story. The Cliffs Notes version reads something like, "There is no big story. There is only whatever fable you can piece together from the seemingly random experiences of life." It is like taking ten novels, each with different characters and plots, and ripping chapter one from the first book, chapter two from the second, and so on. Hoping to enjoy a new story by reading the excised chapters in sequence, you instead find nonsense and confusion. Rather than experiencing each religious story as written, we have ripped random scenes from various subplots in hopes of creating our own scripts.

But it hasn't worked. And many are facing the harsh reality that treating truth claims as "a great spiritual smorgasbord" from which to "help myself, thank you" is another way of saying none of them are true in an ultimate sense.

Yet another writer, Douglas Coupland, coined the term *Generation X* in the title of an earlier bestseller, giving voice to the angst of an entire generation—those whose youth is stained with scenes of the Kennedy and King assassinations, the Vietnam conflict, Watergate, gas lines, and the Iran hostage crisis. Later, in perhaps his most disturbing novel, aptly titled *Life After God*, Coupland tells the story of a young man wandering from one empty experience to the next in search of meaning or purpose in his life, a man who yearns to run so that his spirit can feel the brisk breeze of joy, beauty, clarity, and vitality. But instead he drags a heavy ball of unbelief affixed during childhood.

"I was wondering what was the logical end product of this recent business of my feeling less and less," Coupland's character reflects in response to the soul numbing routine of daily existence. "Is feeling nothing the inevitable end result of believing in nothing? And then I got to feeling frightened—thinking that there might not actually be anything to believe in, in particular. I thought it would be such a sick joke to have to remain alive for decades and not believe in or feel anything."[3]

This shoot of unbelief sprouted from a very specific root: parents who raised their son without religion because they had broken with their own pasts. Having escaped the rigors of Christian commitment, they set their children free. But unbelief, according to one immersed in its hardening mud, does not free. It entombs. It cuts one off from the cool refreshment of clear direction, keeping one on the rat's treadmill rather than the runner's path. Perhaps worst of all, it makes the inviting notion of sincere belief something beyond comprehension—an internal conflict Coupland captures in his character's offensively effective description of Christian media.

And there were Christian radio stations, too, so many many stations, and the voices on them seemed so enthusiastic and committed. They sounded like they sincerely believed in what they were saying, and so for once I decided to pay attention to these stations, trying to figure out what exactly it was they were believing in, trying to understand the notion of Belief...

The radio stations all seemed to be talking about Jesus non-stop, and it seemed to be this crazy orgy of projection, with everyone projecting onto Jesus the antidotes to the things that had gone wrong in their own lives. He is Love. He is Forgiveness. He is Compassion. He is a Wise Career Decision. He is a Child Who Loves Me.

I was feeling a sense of loss as I heard these people. I felt like Jesus was sex—or rather, I felt like I was from another world where sex did not exist and I arrived on Earth and everyone talked about how good sex felt, and showed me their pornography and built their lives around sex, and yet I was forever cut off from the true sexual experience. I did not deny that the existence of Jesus was real to these people—it was merely that I was cut off from their experience in a way that was never connectable.[4]

It is one thing to reject Christianity because you don't understand it. It is another to do so because you can't comprehend the experience of real belief—something made more difficult when parents leave you to decide for yourself among religious options so varied that to claim certainty seems naïvely arrogant at best, dangerous at worst.

I sympathize with the frustration over what seems an endless line of religious perspectives. But there really are not as many as most people think. The modern trend toward relativism has made us lazy by suggesting there are far too many irreconcilable belief systems out there for anyone to compare and contrast. So we throw up our hands and either embrace the one most convenient or ignore them all. We become seekers who will never find.

Hard To Swallow

Christianity claims exclusivity.

CHAPTER 5

Free Agent

"God doesn't care about your specific beliefs.
I think he cares that you are sincerely seeking him.
No matter how wrong you are, he appreciates that."

Ken met me for coffee at the local Barnes & Noble bookstore café. He's a technical analyst in the computer industry who doesn't look the part: brawny build, mustache, goatee, and Bruce Willis haircut. He has a sturdy yet warm presence, reminding me of everyone's uncle.

I learn quickly that his forty-two years have brought some deep hurts, including a difficult divorce that ripped three kids from his daily life—it's probably part of the reason he seems guarded, as though a seed of mistrust has been planted in the fallow ground of a broken heart. His calm, almost stoic personality dictates that Ken doesn't talk much despite having lots to say. He is a self-described unbeliever who turns out to be remarkably well informed about the Christian faith.

When I began examining unbelief I assumed that those who reject Christianity probably do so because they don't get it. They haven't heard or understood the whole story, I reasoned, so they reject a straw man or caricature rather than the genuine article. Ken shattered that assumption, in part because he demonstrated the ability to reference, quote or summarize scriptural stories and themes better than most Christians I've met. He claims to have read the entire Bible three or four times. I can tell there are parts he has read even more than that.

When I ask Ken how he would describe the basic message of Christianity and how it differs from other religions, he hits the nail on the head.

"Christianity is a monotheistic religion that believes in one God and that God is the creator of everything. It teaches that there is right and wrong, and the wrong is identified as sin that needs to be atoned for. Because people are sinning constantly, God made a means of atonement in the form of Jesus Christ who is part of the Trinity. By Jesus dying on the cross despite being sinless, he was paying for everyone else's sin. Everything they had done or ever will do wrong was paid for by that atoning blood. And those who accept that payment are forgiven by God."

Despite a solid grasp of Christian theology, Ken doesn't buy it.

"The Jews hate the Muslims. The Muslims hate the Jews. Christians hate the Jews and Muslims. Nobody can agree on anything; they all seem to hate each other. But there's one thing that they've got in common, and that's God. No matter how wrong those who represent him might be on their own, God is still right—he still exists."

Today, Ken describes himself as a seeker, but he is quick to qualify the term. He is sorting through several faiths, doing his own analysis rather than following the path as defined by the Christian or any other religion. He's a spiritual free agent.

"I still read the Bible. I think it's a great book. I've read about many other religions, but none of the Eastern religions really appeal to me, such as Hindu." Ken believes in a God who looks very much like the monotheistic God of Christianity, Judaism, and Islam. "And it is important to clarify that I'm not opposed to Christianity."

Ken wants to grow spiritually. He doesn't want to block God's work in his life. "But I don't want to just jump in and go along with the crowd."

I assume he means the crowd of devout Christians, many of whom appear to have never checked their locks. He goes on to a topic that touches my own experience growing up in the evangelical church.

"You hear all these grand stories of personal interactions with God: 'God spoke to me,' or 'I had a vision.' And I've never personally encountered anything on these levels. It made me feel that I was missing something or my faith was inadequate."

I can relate. Despite growing up listening to preachers talk about hearing from God, sensing the Spirit, or experiencing an "intimate relationship" with the Almighty, I doubted—sometimes their stories, sometimes my faith. All I knew was that I did not have that kind of drama in my faith life. No voices from heaven. No supernatural sensations. No faith healings. No life-altering encounters. I just bought the gospel as truth, leaving me curious why others seemed to get more direct proof-of-purchase. Ken offers a plausible explanation.

"I just figure there are some people who need that kind of thing so much in order to stay engaged and continue their walk with God," he says. "Some people always have to have a problem to take to God. They aren't happy unless they have a problem. One guy I knew always had a health problem, no matter what. He had a bone spur that needed to be shed or requested prayer and healing for a migraine. It was just constant!"

Ken dislikes those whose spiritual identity becomes wrapped up in what God can fix for them. Of course, God fixing man is central to Christian theology. But some bring the concept too far, giving Ken the impression that Christianity is a crutch for needy people.

He also wonders why so few seem willing to answer tough questions. Ken sincerely wants answers.

"I've always heard that we're not supposed to have a vengeful heart," he says. "If someone does you wrong, you're supposed to turn the other cheek and forgive them, understanding that vengeance is God's work. But then I was reading about Samson and how the last thing he did before bringing down the temple was pray that God would give him strength to bring down his enemies. So, if God doesn't want us to have a vengeful heart, why would he specifically empower Samson to get revenge?"

A good question I've never even asked.

"They would tell me, 'Well, those were God's enemies also and he was doing God's work.' But I still wanted to know why God would go against his own instruction."

Resisting the urge to defend God, I ask for other examples. He describes a Baptist preacher obsessed with proving they never drank wine in the Bible, despite clear statements to the contrary, such as when Jesus turned water into wine. The preacher had alcoholism in his family, so his passion made sense. But it reinforced Ken's suspicion that the church teaches what it wants to be true, regardless of whether the evidence supports it.

What seems to bother Ken more than shallow, weak, or non-answers is the sometimes defensive, sometimes condescending expectation that he should unquestioningly accept whatever explanation he gets. I can relate, having grown up in a church where we were expected to do likewise. I learned pretty quickly that doubting denominational dogma is a no-no. So I kept quiet, something Ken sees no reason to do.

So what parts of Christianity does Ken find hard to swallow?

"I struggle with the idea of original sin," he admits. "I don't understand how I can be held accountable for somebody else's wrongdoing. I think people have their own problems, but sin doesn't pass from one person to another. I've always felt that sin is when you have the opportunity to do something right and you choose not to—like when someone is broken down on the side of the road and you don't stop to help them. It's not necessarily what you do wrong because everybody screws up."

More disturbing than the definition of sin to Ken, however, is its solution.

"The punishment for sin through a blood sacrifice seems to me very primitive. I mean, we chuckle about people throwing the virgin into the volcano—but it is essentially the same thing, taking something pure and sacrificing blood to make up for somebody else's problems. To me that seems like a very primitive method of thinking."

So what alternative does Ken offer?

"People constantly say that you have to pay for your sins. To me, a sin is its own punishment. If you drink too much, your liver dissolves. If you commit adultery, you risk losing your marriage and children. When you murder somebody, you have to carry that guilt to your grave. So to me, sin has its own built-in punishment."

What about justice? Another reason Christianity bothers Ken.

"I believe God is a perfect judge. He can say, 'You're guilty of this sin, and this is your punishment.' But if I become a Christian and just say, 'Jesus is my Lord,' he'll get me off, scot-free, no matter what I've done. That takes away God's ability to be a fair and perfect judge. To me that is contradictory, because a certain group of people are excluded from God's perfect judgment."

Ken doesn't want any "get out of jail free" cards in the game.

Is there a single thing Ken finds most troubling about Christianity? His answer comes with no hesitancy.

"Its exclusive nature," he says. "The fact that it says, 'We're all going to heaven and everybody else is going to hell.' That just seems very wrong. If certain people recognize that understanding, and it empowers them and makes them able to follow God, great! I support them in that. But I don't think that you can put God in a box and say that he's never going to speak to anyone in another voice."

Ken offers the burning bush, Jacob's midnight wrestling match, and Balaam's talking ass as evidence that God can speak to people in other ways if he really wants to reach them. "I look around at the universe, and I don't see God playing by a lot of rules. He's very versatile, very creative."

Kenology

Ken's theology can be summarized as follows:

God is a personal being who created all things, cares about all people, and can talk to us directly if he really wants to. He is a perfect judge who will condemn sin, which Ken defines as hurting others or failing to do good when given the opportunity. He will not let certain people off the hook just because they claim the name of Jesus. Ken celebrates those who believe as he does in one God, whether Christian, Muslim, or Jewish. They are all on different roads to the same eternal goal. He does not buy any religion's claim of exclusivity. All do their best in the journey toward one true God.

"I guess the straw that breaks the camel's back for me," Ken admits, "is that I haven't been convinced Jesus is the Son of God."

So who was he?

"Maybe he was a good teacher. I'm sure he was a good person. But I don't buy the argument Christians offer that he had to be either Lord, lunatic, or liar. He may be legend, like Paul Bunyan or Santa Claus. Saint Nicholas was a real person; but over the centuries that reality has grown into a person who rides a sled each Christmas Eve, bringing gifts to every child on the planet. The same could apply to Mohammed, a very wise man who said and did many wise things. But a prophet of God? That status may have been attributed to him later."

Did Jesus die on a cross? Ken says yes.

Did he rise from the dead?

"That seems more legend than history."

Do unbelievers go to hell?

"I can't see an all-knowing, loving God sending my Muslim grandfather to hell for all eternity. I don't understand what that person could have done in his hundred years on this planet that would deserve an eternity in hell."

What of Jesus' claim to be the only way to heaven?

"I don't believe that he claimed that. That feels like legend."

Is the Bible authoritative or not?

"A little of both. It is a very good source of wisdom in the context of the common mentality of the time. But over the years, it seems there have been embellishments or additions. Two thousand years is a long time for additions to creep in. I view the Bible as containing many things that are good and beneficial. But there are other portions that cause me to doubt."

What traits does Ken see among Christians that would cause belief? Are we needy? Naïve? Or is there some other common characteristic Ken has observed that might drive us toward belief?

"I sense a common desire for God to save or rescue them from some kind of hardship or need."

"Like an injured person needing a crutch?" I ask.

"In some ways, yes. But not in the negative way that is often used. If they need somebody to encourage them and help them along as a focal point, that's great. And I pray to God and ask for help. But my question is, 'What is it *I* need to do?' Christians seem to leave it to God to do all the work for them."

Ken paraphrases an essay by Emerson titled "Self-Reliance" to summarize his own perspective:

> As soon as the man is at one with God, he will not beg. He will then see prayer in all action. The prayer of the farmer kneeling in his field to weed it, the prayer of the rower kneeling with the stroke of his oar, are true prayers heard throughout nature, though for cheap ends.[1]

The farmer doesn't just stand there, helpless, asking God to do something. The farmer's prayer is his work. That, says Ken, defines how he tries to live his own life.

"I pray to God and ask his guidance. But if I sit still and do nothing, why should I expect anything to happen?"

The implication is clear: a common trait that draws many to Christianity is a form of laziness—expecting God to do all the work. Our prayers, be they "plant my crops" or "fix my problem" or "save my soul," suggest an unwillingness to take personal responsibility for our own lives.

Just as I am wrestling to try to understand what motivates unbelief, Ken has tried to categorize reasons for belief. He gives two.

Category one: the unexamined life.

"The vast majority of those who call themselves believers don't know or care why they believe," Ken explains. "They were raised in the church, it was their social upbringing, and they are just following suit. They don't bother to question anything. Ignorance is bliss."

Category two: sincere believers.

"There is another group of believers who are seeking God. And I think that God has used Christianity to speak to them in a way that they can understand. And I love that! God doesn't care about your specific beliefs. I think he cares that you are sincerely seeking him. No matter how wrong you are, he appreciates that. Kind of like getting a homemade Father's Day card from your kid. The drawing is not going to be Rembrandt, but you look at his desire to please you. How can you condemn that?"

How indeed.

Hard To Swallow

Sincerity is not enough.

Bad Impressions

—The OFFENDED—

I've got nothing against God.
It's his fan club I can't stand.

CHAPTER 6

An Awful Taste

"Your mommy is going to hell."

A construction paper Bible verse is tacked slightly off center onto the large bulletin board. A dozen or so miniature chairs sit in a semicircle facing the neatly groomed teacher, her brown hair gathered tightly into a bun in stereotypical church lady fashion. In fact, the entire scene could have come from one of Garrison Keillor's Lake Wobegon sketches, nice Midwestern Lutheran children settling in for a story while grown-ups endure a longer-than-appreciated sermon in the main sanctuary. For most of the kids, yet another forgettable hour in church.

For Wil, a day he will never forget. The day a Sunday school teacher told him, "Your mommy is going to hell." That's something no eight-year-old boy is ready to hear, especially from a near stranger.

Since he doesn't often attend church, Wil feels unaccustomed to the general concept of eternal damnation, or the specific notion that his mommy tops the "condemned" list. The notion adds to the estrangement he already feels as the only kid in class with dark skin. His mother came from the Middle East and grew up in a Muslim home—neither white nor Christian.

Wil attends the class only because his father, raised Lutheran, encourages Wil and his siblings to visit church every now and then. When you live in a small North Dakota town in the 1960s,

occasional church attendance functions as a pass to good standing within their predominantly Lutheran community.

His mother supports the idea. She has never considered herself a devout Muslim, an occasional fast during Ramadan and a
half-hearted effort to avoid pork the extent of her commitment—
nothing as extreme as head coverings or a Mecca pilgrimage.
Wil's mom is a cultural Muslim, the Islamic equivalent of a
Catholic who attends Christmas and Easter mass but who hasn't
confessed in years. Her casual religious commitment didn't impel
her to marry a Muslim; she chose a lapsed Lutheran instead.
Mom and dad agreed they would not force their Christian or
Muslim background into Wil's life. They consider spirituality
something everyone should investigate on their own before making a decision.

So, at eight years old, Wil decided. He stopped attending the
church that so casually damned his mommy's eternal soul.

Years later, Wil tells me, he re-entered the Christian scene in
less-than-ideal circumstances. As a senior in high school, his girl-
friend became pregnant. Trying to do the right thing, he decided
to marry. There was just one problem: the bride wanted a church
wedding—her *Lutheran* church.

"Unless you are willing to convert from . . . from . . ." An
awkward pause suggested the minister didn't exactly know Wil's
religion. Truth be known, he had none. "Anyway, you must go
through confirmation and baptism to join this church before I
can perform the ceremony." But the minister's tone sounded
more antagonistic than welcoming, a bit like a threat. To Wil, little seemed to have changed at the church since he was a kid sitting in Sunday school.

They had the wedding elsewhere.

⌯

"It's a girl!" Three words turned an embarrassing mistake into a
cause for celebration. Little Emily's birth brought a sense of pur-

pose into Wil's young life. But it also forced another conversation with the Lutheran minister. Wil's wife really wanted their daughter baptized into the faith.

"We baptize only the children of members in good standing," the minister said as he once more pulled out the knife. "So unless you are willing to convert, I can't baptize your daughter." Wil, always a bit mule headed, digs in his heels when pushed.

Unlike some less confrontational ministers, this one decided to shoot straight. "Do you understand that if your daughter dies today, she is going to burn in hell forever because you're being stubborn!"

The same church that had condemned his mother to hell was now doing the same to his daughter, and laying the blame on Wil's unbelieving shoulders.

Two more kids came along, another daughter and a son. They brought them to a different church, hoping to have them baptized. But the message remained the same: "We can't baptize children unless both of the parents are believers and members of the church." Same song, second and third verse.

After attempt number three, Wil pointed his fed-up finger of condemnation in the other direction: "You are the people who are given the responsibility within the church to baptize, and you don't want to because you'd rather fill the pews than fulfill God's word! So you're the ones responsible for these children burning in hell because you won't do it. I'm not stopping you. You just don't want to do it because I won't join the fun!"

And for the third time, Wil walked away from church with a bad taste in his mouth.

⤫

Several years and one nasty divorce later, Wil began to reflect on his life: early thirties, a successful computer analyst career, college educated, and a few significant life experiences, some of which he would rather forget. Still, on the whole, Wil considered himself pretty well-rounded—with one glaring exception.

"I had avoided my spiritual life," he said. "I hadn't investigated it at all."

So what did he do about it?

"Being an avid reader, I began by diving into books. I'm the kind of person who likes to do some personal investigation, compile whatever questions I might have."

Most of his "investigation" centered on reading the Bible and the Koran, something one might expect, considering Wil's Lutheran and Muslim parents.

"I wanted to know more about what my parents and grandparents were into. What was it that motivated them? What were they basing their faith on? I wanted to see if any of it made sense to me or if none of it made sense to me."

During this two-year process, Wil became interested in a lady heavily involved with the Assembly of God church. That relationship opened his eyes to a Christian subculture very different from the one he had encountered among Lutherans. Forget liturgy and confirmation! This world was all about praise and celebration.

For his very first service, Wil attended an old-fashioned, holy roller camp meeting, complete with lots of shouting and other (and stranger) emotional outbursts. "It's not like this all the time," came the apologetic explanation of his girlfriend and others, apparently recognizing how frightening the whole experience might seem to a more reserved newcomer like Wil.

"It wasn't always like that, but it was always something," Wil said, "especially after I made a profession of faith." A profession Wil admits had been motivated by the desire to maintain his relationship with a Christian girlfriend. Hoping to keep the relationship smooth and moving forward, Wil prayed an insincere prayer during a meeting in the pastor's office. The excited minister believed he was leading a sinner to salvation, unaware that it was the sinner doing the leading (or rather, *mis*leading).

Before too long his clever plot unraveled. A lady in this church, claiming to have the gift of prophecy, cornered Wil's girl-friend in the parking lot and told her that God had given her a vision telling her that Wil was a "dark and evil" person. In this subculture of Christianity, one doesn't simply ignore a prophetic word, because the church teaches they can come from the Lord. So the young woman took the warning seriously, severely curb-ing Wil's hopes for romantic bliss.

"Why doesn't the church oppose this lady saying stuff like that?" Wil wonders aloud. "When they're born again, all things are made new. But when I'm born again, I get to be dark and evil. What's up with that?"

I find it difficult to feel sorry for him. After all, he did pray the sinner's prayer in order to get a girl. Still, his offense seems more "desperate and sneaky" than "dark and evil."

Either way, that became the beginning of the end for Wil's relationship, both with the girl and with the church.

"I was real angry for a while," he remembers. "But then I thought, *I can't blame God for what these people do. I need to give him a chance.*"

Many would have abandoned their quest after either one of the Lutheran or Assembly offenses. To his credit, Wil felt willing to give Christianity three full swings before calling it out.

His next pitch: the Baptists.

Recognizing that he had made a Christian commitment for the wrong reason, Wil thought he should take a deeper look to see if he could make it for the right reasons. Returning to his list of questions compiled while reading the Bible, he brought his intel-lectual curiosity into a congregation not quite up to the challenge.

"Maybe it's just bad luck," he muses, "but the Baptist church I went to was equally shallow and narrow-minded, with their lit-tle blinders on. They said that they welcomed questions. But whenever you asked one that they weren't comfortable with, you'd get this canned, 'You just have to accept it and have faith' answer."

Not good enough for a man who, as a technical analyst, is used to due diligence before launch. A "measure twice, cut once" kind of guy.

Wil has always been an analytical person, picking things apart to see how they work. In his view, if it works, then it must be right. But if it doesn't work, then something must be wrong. He naturally applied such thinking to the Bible. If the Bible says, "This is the way it works," but the end results don't surface in real life—or if God doesn't appear to be working the way the Bible says he should be—then it must not be right.

So Wil asked questions of "Bible-believing Baptists." After all, they seem to emphasize Bible teaching over most Christian denominations. Surely they should be able to handle his list.

"You can't understand until you believe"—that was their all-too-common response. A square peg that didn't fit his mind's round hole.

"I just thought it ridiculous!" declares Wil. "During the first thirty-some years of my life, every exposure to Christianity has been negative."

Third swing. Third miss. Called out.

"A pastor friend of mine said there are two reasons people will or will not come to church," Wil summarizes. "Either they've met a Christian, or they've met a Christian. I think that is what it comes down to for me. Every church seems to have a certain number of hoops you have to jump through, whether they know it or not, whether they want them or not. They are still there. The Charismatic church wants you to fall on the floor and speak in tongues. The Lutheran church wants you to go through communion the way they do it. The whole pursuit becomes a very uncomfortable adventure when it should be joyful."

"Do you plan to give it another try?" I ask.

"The people in the church I was attending when I made a profession of faith undid any good feelings I would ever have about my decision," Wil replies. "Some people don't just want you to accept God, but accept him the way they do because that's what they are comfortable with. Others I consider very good Christians and I really do support them in their faith. I'm not opposed to it. It's just that I'm not going to jump in and then try to figure it out like I did before. I won't do that again."

Wil has had some very disappointing life experiences and ugly encounters with those who claim Christianity. Both have moved him away from belief, away from the church. Others who have gone through similar or even more difficult experiences hold strong faith. I end our time together by asking Wil if he can explain what makes the difference.

"I guess some people are just gluttons for punishment!" he says.

We share a knowing laugh.

Hard To Swallow

Christians are unkind.

CHAPTER 7

To Hell with You!

"So anyone who doesn't believe the way you do
is going to hell?"

How can you believe that?"

The conversation hadn't gone as I had hoped. What was supposed to be a loving invitation for my mother-in-law to accept Jesus as her personal Savior became twisted into something else entirely. I'd thrown the lifeline to a drowning loved one, only to have her get tangled up in its line. The rope intended to rescue somehow got all wrapped around her neck. Was my toss or her struggle to blame?

"So anyone who doesn't believe the way you do is going to hell?" Her words squeezed through clenched teeth, revealing intensity forced under control. Clearly, the conversation had tapped a long emotional history with regard to Christianity. After all, the only "H" word I'd mentioned was heaven.

"How can you believe I am going to hell?" Tears of angry indignation flowed while I fumbled to redeem the conversation. But we had long passed the point of sharing "the good news of the gospel." No matter what I said, she remained fixed on one thought: Kurt is one of those insensitive Christians who believes she is condemned to eternal damnation.

Olive had good reason to react. We met when I began dating her daughter, Olivia. I became a permanent fixture in her life when I married into the family, a family understandably leery of those who wear the label "Christian."

Only a few months before our little chat, Olive had one of the most offensive confrontations imaginable, the kind that would give any unbeliever nightmares. She hesitantly accepted an invitation to a chapel service at the Baptist college her daughter attended, despite her uneasiness about the high pressure evangelism she had come to expect from fundamentalists. Olive had already rejected one form of Christianity, the Catholicism of her childhood. She had no interest in accepting another. And even if she had, it wouldn't be the Bible-thumping, hellfire-and-brimstone variety her daughter had somehow become caught up in. But Olivia was taking part in a special musical performance, and she really wanted her mother to come. How can a parent say no? So Olive came and sat in the very back of the auditorium, hoping to make a quick exit.

Neither mother nor daughter realized that there had been a setup. The special chapel speaker that day was an old-style evangelist, the sort that took no prisoners. He believed all is fair in love, war, and evangelism. Thanks to a tip from one of Olivia's concerned fellow students, he knew an unbelieving mother would be in the audience. So he did the unthinkable. After proclaiming the hard truth of hell and the glorious hope of heaven, he pointed the verbal spotlight directly on Olive.

"I've been told that there is a mother here today who came to see her daughter perform."

The speaker's words sent a chill of cold terror darting through Olivia's body. *How does he know? Why in the world would he say such a thing from the platform?* And what would he say next?

"Mom, you have a lovely child who desperately wants you to accept Jesus as your Lord and Savior."

Olivia could do nothing. Her mother sat a dozen or more rows away; she had no way to explain that this was neither her idea nor doing. So she endured, hoping it would end soon.

"Don't you think it is time that you finally submit to the prompting of God's Spirit and accept the gift of salvation he offers?"

After a few more appeals to Olive and any other "lost" in the crowd, the preacher wrapped up his portion of the service. Relieved the tense ordeal had finally ended, Olivia joined her fellow singers on stage to perform one final number. Then came the hard part, repairing the damage with Mom.

Unbelievably, things went from bad to worse. Much worse.

Just as Olivia reached her mother to begin post-service small talk before easing into an apology, the guest preacher approached in order to raise the bar with a direct, personal confrontation. Both Olivia and Mom got that deer-in-the-headlights look as he began a process of rapid-fire evangelism at point-blank range. Emotions and defenses already high, the conversation quickly escalated. The preacher, visibly frustrated by Mom's stubborn resistance to the gospel, pulled out the heavy artillery.

"Madam, do you realize that if you die you will never see your daughter again, because she will be in heaven and you will be in hell?"

Both Mom and daughter burst into tears, Mom out of indignant rage, daughter out of perplexed shock. Years of gentle, loving attempts to show Jesus' love suddenly got blown out of the water by "kick ass" evangelism.

No wonder Olive resists any attempt on the part of Christians to "share the good news." Even if her heart wanted to know, her mind can't help recalling Rambo the preacher. Or she suspects an evangelistic ambush, all designed to overwhelm her with one key message: "Olive, you are going to hell!"

She recalls a similar message growing up in a strict Catholic home. Olive tried to be a good girl, tried to follow the prescribed order of faith: mass, confession, rosary, and the rest. But something seemed askew. The faith that claimed to be the truth and the light failed to dispel the lies and darkness dominating her home. Being devout certainly hadn't helped her father kick the bottle. Nor had it prevented her brother Tom's apparent suicide. Mother wore an air of superiority reflecting anything but the spirit of a Lord "meek, lowly, and humble of heart." She disliked blacks, Jews, and Protestants. But then, so did most of her devout friends.

Olive found herself reacting against the faith of her parents. Not so much because she disagreed with or even understood its creeds, but because it was theirs. Yet leaving the Catholic church is the spiritual equivalent of jumping from a plane without a parachute. No matter how much fun you may have on the way down, you eventually reach bottom, where Dante's inferno awaits.

Nonetheless, Olive left the church. But its dogma never left her, including the nagging awareness that one cannot walk away with impunity. Even though she told herself she no longer believed in hell, it pursued her through the belief of others: father, mother, brother, and years later, daughter.

I've learned the hard way that it is important to listen before you speak when discussing faith. I wish I had known more of the offenses perpetrated on Olive before we talked. I wish I knew of her hell hang-up before speaking of heaven. It would have been nice to know that no matter what I said, what she heard would first squeeze through a filter of bad experiences and conversations, none of which had painted an attractive picture of Christian belief.

You see, sometimes, when Christians say, "Jesus loves you," all others can hear is, "To hell with you!"

Hard To Swallow

Confrontational evangelism.

CHAPTER 8

Wandering

"I don't like preachers who yell."

My interview with Jo Anne brought me back in time, awakening pleasant echoes of my own religious upbringing: a southern gospel quartet performing energetic tunes in tight, bouncing harmony; the rhythmic, almost poetic form of preaching that stirred the soul more than engaged the mind; an altar call at the end of each sermon when the preacher appealed to those needing salvation or rededication to "walk the aisle" while the congregation sang each verse of "Just As I Am." Like Jo Anne, I miss parts of the distinctively Baptist subculture that defined my youth.

Decades later, you might never guess by looking at her that Jo Anne once stood on street corners handing out gospel tracts, or entered prisons to help lead inmate church services—part of her training during three semesters at a strict Bible college. You might not guess she taught a Sunday school class when her kids were young. With a charming blend of sixty-something sophistication and new age hip, Jo Anne does not fit the part.

She admits feeling nervous about our meeting because the question I pose, "Why is Christianity so hard to swallow?" represents a lifetime struggle. Jo Anne envies the experience of those who embrace Christianity as a natural, normal part of life. Her story draws me into the stereotypical world of hellfire-and-brimstone preaching and guilt-inducing legalism. Several snap-shots tell the tale of Jo Anne's journey.

At thirteen, Jo Anne felt lifestyle whiplash after her older brother "surrendered to preach." The family had been nominal churchgoers, able to take most sermons with a grain of salt. Not anymore. Big brother became the family thought and behavior police: no more dancing, playing cards, going to picture shows, or "mixed bathing" (allowing boys and girls to swim in the same pool together). So, in the name of holy living, fun was outlawed. Mother could not have been more proud and supportive of her son's newfound zeal, and eventually he went on to become a "big-time preacher" with a large ministry.

At about fifteen years of age, Jo Anne participated in a youth group mission to Hispanic and black families on the other side of her very segregated town: "We were delivering donated coats to their homes, and I was deeply saddened by the devastating poverty I saw. One week later, a member of the church deacon board announced the exciting news that the church had paid off the sixty-thousand-dollar stained glass enhancement project. It just felt wrong."

Later that summer, an evangelist came to town for the annual tent revival—always a big event that included Vacation Bible School for the children. Jo Anne volunteered to help the little kids with crafts, giving her an opportunity to observe the evangelist in another context. For some reason, he gave her the creeps. One afternoon when the evangelist offered to drive Jo Anne home, she declined, wary of getting into the car alone with him.

After a short stint in Bible college—the same school her "high flying" preacher brother attended—Jo Anne married a man she met in church. He entered the Air Force, largely at her urging, in order to escape West Texas. While stationed in England, Jo Anne discovered the liturgical environment of the Church of England. It made her uncomfortable, so she took a vacation from church involvement until returning Stateside where she took their four kids to a mainline Protestant congregation where she ended up teaching Sunday school.

Jo Anne can't really pinpoint when she started drifting away from church life. Perhaps it happened during their second post in England, or when her husband went to Vietnam, or when he returned a heavy drinker. Maybe it was all of the above. Whatever the reasons, her family gradually disengaged, to the point that church became the place for holidays, weddings, or funerals.

I find it telling what people do and don't remember. Jo Anne clearly recalls specific snapshots of the worst moments of her church experience. She has no trouble detailing this or that offense—many of them tied to her brother, the overbearing, successful preacher. But she can't recall an intentional decision to leave an active life of faith. The drift from belief feels ambiguous, with only a few loose recollections to chronicle the voyage.

Today, Jo Anne wanders in and out of an occasional church service, "even the Catholic chapel around the corner from my house," she adds with some self-congratulation, pleased by the broad-mindedness achieved. "I pray and read the Bible several times per week. I prefer the New Testament. I don't read the Old Testament much, other than Psalm 23. I've always been a searcher."

How would Jo Anne describe her current religious status?

"I would definitely say that I'm Christian, but not in the traditional sense."

Why untraditional?

"I don't like church. But I also feel guilty for not attending, especially on Sunday mornings."

Then why don't you go?

"I don't like preachers who yell. I don't like big churches. I don't like people raising their hands because it reminds me of those holy rollers from my youth. I don't like liturgical services because they feel too cold and stiff." In other words, she didn't like any of the churches she has tried.

Still, it bothers Jo Anne that her grandchildren don't attend church, since "every well-rounded person should be familiar with the Bible." She clearly sees a value in church. I prod further, hoping to discover what has caused such a conflicted response.

"Why do you let service style issues get in your way?"

"I wonder sometimes," she replies. "Especially since I consider myself an open-minded person."

After a reflective pause, Jo Anne attempts to put into words what before she had only felt. "I can't go along with the guilt peddling," she begins. "And I find it offensive that, in my experience, most Christians are very critical and judgmental of others."

When I ask for examples, her preacher brother becomes Exhibit A. "Neither he nor his wife have a good word to say about anyone. And he lives in a gated community!"

Clearly, intense emotion bubbles below the surface, a disgust and disdain that must feed Jo Anne's negative impression of confident Christianity.

"I guess I have problems with Christians who are so sure. Aren't we all seeking? I know I have been."

"What do you think is behind that confidence?" I ask.

"I think in most cases it is because they blindly accept it without really thinking it through. I want to go at this intellectually, making sure it is thought through and struggled through."

"Struggled" is the key word for Jo Anne. If someone seems unsure, she will listen. If they boldly proclaim with confidence, she won't. It troubles her when believers confidently proclaim Christianity as the only way, something I gather big brother does while pounding his pulpit.

Diving into my list of questions, I discover just how "non-traditional" Jo Anne's Christianity turned out.

"How do you define Christianity?"

"The essence of Christian belief is love. I believe love can conquer everything." While certain the Beatles would concur, I had hoped for more than bumper sticker slogans.

"Forgiveness is a big part of it. God sent his Son to earth to die for our sins, making the ultimate sacrifice," Jo Anne adds, assuring me she retains a whisper of orthodoxy.

"How would you describe God?" I continue.

"God is more like a presence within me, a Spirit. And I believe that he could come in different forms to us." An answer suggesting some influence from eastern religions.

What does Jo Anne find most troubling about traditional Christian belief?

"The idea that Hindus, Jews, and those who embrace other religions won't have life after death because they believe differently." Her concern for others seems genuine. "That is where I get stuck."

How does Jo Anne reconcile Jesus' statements claiming to be the only way with this concern?

"I can't reconcile the two," Jo Anne reluctantly confesses. "And I struggle with people who accept it so blindly. I guess I have a hard time condemning anyone to hell."

Who doesn't? But some still believe Jesus' claim. Does she?

"I'm not sure he said it," she says, an uncertainty she hopes to preserve.

"Bottom line, why do you struggle with Christianity?" In my final question I want to uncover the root of Jo Anne's discomfort with the faith.

"I guess I'm too tenderhearted," she replies. "My struggle is that to totally believe all that Christianity teaches, it scares me. Possibly because I've had so many bad experiences with Christians. I don't want to be like that."

As we conclude our time, I wonder how differently Jo Anne's "search" might have turned out if big brother had sold cars rather than become a "big time preacher." Clearly, he is a major source of her indignation. One thing seems certain: Jo Anne never wants to find what he has, lest she become what he is.

Hard To Swallow

Christians seem too certain.

Little Interest

—The APATHETIC—

*Just because I don't care
doesn't mean I don't understand.*

BUMPER STICKER

CHAPTER 9

A Theory Blown

"I don't see the lines between the religions. . . .
They all think they are right. They all seem intolerant."

I began my research for this book with several hypotheses, including the notion that unbelief is somehow tied to a lack of education or intelligence. If one lives an examined life, I thought, he or she will eventually realize the compelling nature of Christian understanding. On the other hand, more emotional and reactive people who never invest the time or energy to think through foundational questions might reject Christian belief out of simple ignorance or an inability to comprehend its implications.

This theory, of course, left me with at least two problems. First, Jesus told us to come to him as a little child, not as a PhD candidate. Most who believe, do so while young and uneducated, not old and studied. Second, a whole lot of highly educated people reject Christianity, most notably among the academic elite teaching in the finest universities.

I dismissed the high ratio of educated unbelievers as the unfortunate effect of intellectual arrogance. After all, the Bible is filled with warnings against pride. Pride destroys our capacity for true learning, because only the humble can accept instruction. I recall Socrates being placed on trial for exposing this unfortunate tendency among the intellectual elite of his day. So, my theory remained intact.

That is, until my interview with an intelligent, yet humble unbeliever named Chris.

I've known Chris for several years, more as an acquaintance than a friend. I find him intriguing because he projects a persona that seems both sharp and unassuming. Born, raised, and educated in England, Chris moved to America because he fetched a high price in the computer industry—in other words, one smart cookie. Because he had rejected Christianity apparently on intellectual grounds, I felt surprised that he didn't seem to have the swagger of intellectual arrogance. Was Chris the exception to my theory that would prove the rule, or the rule that would blow my theory?

It turns out that Chris once shared my theory, albeit in reverse. I assumed unbelief a symptom of ignorance; he assumed ignorance the cause of belief.

"When I was in high school," the now forty-something Chris recalls, "I was head and shoulders above everyone else intellectually, making it easy to view the religiously devout as simpletons willing to accept easy answers. But when I went to Oxford University, it was the other way around. I moved near the bottom of the intelligence hierarchy. Yet there was a much higher ratio of religious people there. That was an eye opener for me. Some of the people at Oxford were much smarter than I could ever hope to be, yet they believed in God. That is when I realized that something other than intelligence is going on here."

Chris' humble acknowledgment exposes my own pride, arrogantly assuming that I believe because I am smarter than others.

"One of my best friends at University shocked me when I found out just how religious he was—and still is," Chris continues. "I don't recall his specific religious affiliation, but I think it was a Protestant denomination."

Chris' inability to identify this or that version of Christianity does not surprise me. He has never grown all that interested in particular shades of what seems one big blur. "I don't see the lines between the religions," he admits. "They all seem to have the same issues, so far as I'm concerned. They all think they are right. They all seem intolerant. And they're all willing to fight for it, with the possible exception of Buddhism."

Chris rattles off several examples of his point, including the never-ending holy wars of the Middle East, the "path of destruction" the Roman church left behind over the centuries, and the conflict in Northern Ireland between Protestants and Catholics. "That entire fight is based on religion," he reflects. "How can they, on one hand, embrace a religion that teaches tolerance and forgiveness, while on the other hand blow up somebody's family or bomb a pub? I remember seeing a photograph taken moments before an IRA car bombing in a busy market square one Saturday morning. This sweet little girl was sitting on her daddy's shoulder while others innocently walked around with shopping bags. That photo brought home the reality of what these people were doing, because that girl and those people were blown to bits only a few seconds later."

I sense in Chris' voice and see in his eyes the kind of outrage that gripped my own heart while watching images of the September 11 collapse of the World Trade Center. I wondered what kind of religiously zealous madmen would do such a horrible thing in the name of God. In my case, I relegated such behavior to fanatical Muslims. But to Chris, religion itself is the problem. Christianity included.

Confident Uncertainty

So how does Chris describe himself from a religious perspective?

"I am an agnostic," he says. "I wouldn't say that I'm an atheist, because I'm not really sure. But if I had to put money on it, I'd put a lot of money against!" Hard on convinced believers, Chris is equally hard on those who confidently declare God to be mere fantasy. "To me, being an atheist is as illogical as belief, because there's no proof either way."

When asked to summarize the basic tenets of Christian belief, Chris does a fairly good job of capturing the key ideas.

"There was this guy named Jesus Christ who lived a few millennia ago whose philosophy is pretty well documented, based upon his teachings about love, tolerance, and forgiveness. After his death, a following developed. The manner of his death had a lot to do with it. He was murdered for his beliefs by the government of the day, which saw his influence among the people as a threat."

In England, the state requires one hour per week of religious instruction. Chris relies heavily upon bits and pieces of those early lessons as he continues. "It is said that three days after he was murdered, Jesus reappeared to people close to him and gave them a message about his God—an all-seeing, all-being, ubiquitous, all-powerful influence who created us. To be a Christian, you must believe that these things happened by simply being told it happened; that's called faith."

Resisting the urge to jump in and clarify the meaning of faith, I listen as Chris reveals a nasty impression of church history.

"As time went on the movement grew, and eventually became corrupt itself as people saw this religion as a way to control people, to stop them from thinking their own thoughts. Various churches and religions emerged, leading to the many sects of Christianity we have today. But I think they are all based upon these very simple ideas of forgiveness, tolerance, and love."

After his brief, fairly accurate attempt to explain the difference between the Old and New Testament Scriptures, I ask Chris to react to several ideas associated with Christian belief.

God created the world.

"That is very, very unlikely," he retorts.

Why?

"Where's the evidence?"

Human beings are sinful beings.

"Absolutely. I see plenty of evidence for that." After listening to a few examples of man's inhumanity to man, I ask Chris the basis upon which he calls one behavior wrong and another right. A very good question, he muses. But he sees no connection to whether God exists.

Jesus claimed to be the Son of God.

"I would bet that he said that, if making a wager."

He died on a cross.

"I am quite confident on that one. Yes."

He rose from the dead.

"The evidence seems weak. It happened so long ago and was so poorly documented, with differing accounts. So I'd worry about my money if betting on that one."

Starting to feel like I am in Las Vegas rather than having a religious discussion, I move on to the next concept.

Unbelievers suffer eternal damnation.

"I just laugh at the concept," snaps Chris. "Ideas like that come from the Catholic church trying to control people. My grandmother was scared as hell of that idea because she had a child who died before he was christened. She believed the child went to purgatory. Disgusting!"

How does Chris perceive those who try to convert him?

"My roommate in University once said he was praying for me, hoping that I would believe before I die. But on the whole, we were very respectful of each other's views. I didn't ask, 'How can you believe this stuff, it's nothing but a fairy tale.' Nor did he say, 'You're going to hell if you don't believe.'"

Still, his friend had an impact.

"I found his concern for me touching."

I ask whether he found it touching, like a child worried that you won't receive presents from Santa because you are being naughty, or touching, like a friend trying to save you from real harm?

"I appreciated his concern," Chris responds. "But I was pretty confident he was wrong in his belief."

So, it's touching, like the child worried about Santa—which makes sense, in light of the thing Chris finds most odd about Christian belief.

"Well, belief in a God has never made much sense to me. To say God created the universe begs the question of who made God."

"So what is your view of beginnings, of first cause?" I prod.

"That hasn't been solved yet. But there are great mathematical minds working on that question, and we are closer to understanding than ever before. We might not figure it out in our lifetimes, but we are making progress." Chris continues with some passion, energized by a topic he has spent a great deal of time exploring. He dives deep, rattling off phrases like "unified theory of physics" and "quantum mechanics," concepts I vaguely recall from a popular book I read in the late 1980s by Stephen Hawking titled *A Brief History of Time*. Mentioning the title gets me back into the conversation as Chris reflects on the man who held Sir Isaac Newton's chair as Professor of Mathematics at Cambridge University.

"It is interesting," Chris reflects, "that Hawking seems to find no contradiction between pursuing a unifying theory for how the universe began and belief in God."

Apparently, I had an ally in Hawking. But I am not trying to provide Chris with evidence of my view. I want to discover why he doesn't seem to care whether that evidence exists. How can someone so interested in the Big Bang's explosion care so little about who might have lit the fuse?

Chris shows no concern for questions that, in his view, fall outside human comprehension. How did we get here? What is our purpose? Let someone else chase after such inexplicable mysteries. Chris prefers the pragmatic, tangible benefits of sticking to the scientific method: observe, develop a theory, test that theory using observation, etc.

As if using half a pair of binoculars but peering with only one eye through the single lens of rationalism, he sees a two-dimensional image explaining the mechanics of things. The other lens, the lens of reason, could reveal the three-dimensional depth and richness available when one opens both eyes to perceive the Maker of things.

But then, Chris doesn't much care about discovering the Maker of things. "Have you ever seriously examined whether Christianity is true?" I inquire, perplexed by what seems near total indifference.

"Not voluntarily," Chris confesses. "Other than the lesson per week I received from ages six to sixteen in school, I haven't studied these matters. I guess I've had so little confidence that it would reveal anything meaningful to me, I never went down that path." In other words, "Why bother?" I've often wondered why many "agnostics" parrot tired clichés against belief rather than seriously engaging the topic. Chris considers Christianity hard to swallow because he sees no evidence for the existence of a God. And yet, he admits having never examined what I see as a mountain of evidence.

What is going on here? This is a man with a successful career in a complicated field, who graduated from one of the most prestigious universities on the planet, and recently ran a grueling marathon all the way to the top of Pikes Peak in the Rocky Mountains. Not to mention reading quantum physics in his spare time! It is difficult to write off his indifference to mere sloth. Laziness is not in his nature. So why doesn't he investigate such important questions further?

It comes down to a single word: apathy. Chris, like countless others, has no interest in what Christianity proclaims or offers. He doesn't hate it. And since he never accepted it, he hasn't disowned it. He has simply ignored it, disregarding whatever claims it might make on his time and attention. A non-issue.

I recall a scene from that great film *Casablanca*, starring Humphrey Bogart. When the obnoxious Ugarte invites himself to Rick's table for some unwelcome chatter, Rick becomes visibly annoyed.

"You despise me, don't you?" Ugarte asks.

"Well," responds Rick, "if I gave you any thought, I probably would."

Chris doesn't despise God. He just doesn't give him any thought.

Thus, a new theory replaces the old. It is possible for highly intelligent, humble people to reject Christianity without much trouble. They aren't ignorant. They aren't arrogant. They simply don't care.

Hard To Swallow

There's no proof either way.

CHAPTER **10**

No Nonsense

"Perhaps more than anything,
I find the fervor of Christians offensive."

After five minutes with Katherine, I pegged her as a no-nonsense kind of gal. Late forties, professional demeanor and attire, she carries herself with a controlled confidence that nearly touches the line between cordial and intimidating. It does not surprise me to learn Katherine has a Master's degree in public administration and is CEO of her company. She sets the course, gives the orders, hires and fires, and pays the bills. She looks visibly uncomfortable as I begin the interview, a woman more accustomed to asking tough questions than answering them.

Katherine wonders why she is here. (A mutual friend recommended that we talk. He considers her an unbeliever, which bothers Katherine.)

"I feel like I am guided by God on a daily basis," she begins. "I pray on a daily basis. I think of myself as a Christian. Yet others consider me a non-believer. I do have a hard time with the 'born again' concept, as opposed to what I would call Christian." Katherine does not participate in any sort of religious activities or attend church. "I guess I would describe myself as less intense about Christianity. I am much more laid back about it, which may or may not be acceptable."

97

The most "intense" Katherine has ever been about the faith occurred during childhood—which isn't saying much, since her Presbyterian family attended church only sporadically. You could count on two fingers the family's annual participation.

"I got the Easter story down!" she laughs.

But pain flows under the surface. Katherine's father, formerly devout, became angry at God after his then-twelve-year-old son died. Katherine, six at the time, didn't understand much of what transpired. One thing is certain, however: "We experienced a lot of difficulty, and the family's faith foundation fell apart."

Katherine's other brother later became what she calls a "born-again Christian," revealing a possible root to what seems a defensive reaction to the concept. "But that is something he chose after leaving the house."

Several non-verbal signals suggest Katherine is ready to progress to the next item on the agenda. We will not be diving into memories or exploring the emotional trauma of childhood experiences. Those matters have been filed away for decades; let's keep them where they belong.

"I think I'm fairly educated," Katherine responds to my inquiry about her exposure to Christianity. "I've read the Bible. And I've read the entire *Left Behind* series about the end of the world." I react with surprise, since Katherine doesn't seem the typical fan of apocalyptic fiction.

Her résumé complete, I ask Katherine to summarize her understanding of the basic tenets of Christianity.

"It is very similar to other religions, with the big differences being the Bible and the teachings of Christ as the one and only path to God. Most other religions have different paths to God, related to your performance, your goodness, etc. Christianity does not believe that you can get to heaven by good works alone. You have to accept Christ, believe that he died for your sins and that he is the one Savior."

Clearly she has been exposed to a particularly evangelical presentation of the gospel, perhaps by her born-again brother. "Of course, many religions are offshoots of Christianity, such as the Mormons, Jehovah's Witnesses, and Catholics." Apparently, Katherine's key influences have described Catholicism as a cult.

"Christianity is similar to most religions," she continues, "by teaching that you should do your best to avoid sin—bad works, anything not acceptable as stated in the Bible, such as lying, cheating, stealing, killing, adultery, hurting others. The basic rules are much the same across religions."

Katherine believes the core of Christianity teaches us to be good, avoid sin, and recognize Christ as the one way to heaven.

"Do you believe what you just explained?" I ask, trying to determine whether Katherine is repeating her brother's sales pitch or summarizing a faith she has embraced.

"I do," Katherine admits. "But then I falter from time to time. I have difficulty, not so much with Christianity as with people who call themselves Christians. I know that's not God's fault; you can't blame him for that."

Or can you? I get the impression Katherine thinks God is slack in his hiring practices.

"Bumper stickers like, 'I'm not perfect, I'm just forgiven,' offend me. There is an arrogance in Christianity that I don't think Jesus would want at all."

I don't particularly like that bumper sticker either, but I find it odd that Katherine perceives arrogance in its message. As the interview continues, I discover what may be the real root of her criticism.

A Distasteful Fervor

"Perhaps more than anything," Katherine explains, "I find the fervor of Christians offensive. It doesn't fit my personality, since I consider spiritual beliefs something private."

Katherine tells of several firsthand encounters she found troubling, starting with the Victory Outreach Chapel Christmas
drama. Fairly entertaining, but, in her words, "The reason for it
was to have people come to the front at the end and get 'saved.'
I am very uncomfortable with that approach. To me, it is much
more personal, and that type of thing makes it feel like selling
used cars."

And then there was her visit to a little church where a man gave
his conversion testimony. "He talked about his repeated failings as
a sinner, and how we human beings are such insignificant creatures, like little grasshoppers in the field compared to Christ. Why
can't Christianity be ego-strengthening instead of ego-bashing?"

Katherine feels equally unimpressed by the liturgical tradition.
"If you go to the Catholic Church, you've got to learn all the rituals, or else you look like an idiot." And looking like an idiot
seems something this together, controlled woman tries to avoid.
"I attended a Catholic service with a friend in high school, and
it turned out to be one of the most humiliating experiences of my
life. When do you kneel? When do you eat the cookie?"

During her teenage years Katherine became fairly serious
about Christianity, even attending church with a close friend
whose mother routinely "spoke in tongues." She found the
charismatic culture a bit scary—overboard and too intense.

I begin piecing the picture together. Katherine grew up in a
family that attended church twice per year, maintaining an ever-
so-slight connection to her parents' faith tradition. They didn't
talk about religion, maintaining a safe detachment from its more
serious demands. They considered Christianity something that
civilized people include in their life portfolio.

As an adult, Katherine's big brother had some sort of conversion experience, after which he began talking too much about
his own faith and pushing her to become born again. Put off by
the confrontational, passionate nature of a religion Katherine rel-
egates to moral guidance and holiday traditions, she remains

turned off by those who take this stuff so seriously. Still, Katherine resents being categorized among those who reject Christianity. She hasn't rejected it; she just doesn't need it.

Katherine believes God created the world, despite struggling with the notion of a literal, six-day creation. She agrees that God is a loving, personal Father, that we are a bunch of sinners in need of mercy, and that Jesus died and rose from the dead three days later. Whether Jesus is the only way to heaven gives Katherine a more difficult time.

"I have a hard time with that one," she confesses. "And the idea that unbelievers go to hell. Both seem to conflict with the idea of a loving God. It just goes against everything else in the philosophy. A just, loving, and kind God doesn't just 'off' people who don't get it."

"I guess I wonder why God wouldn't spell it out so we have it much clearer," Katherine admits when asked her level of confidence in the faith. "I would like to have a much better understanding of the whole thing."

"How far have you gone in pursuing that understanding?" I ask.

"Not very," she acknowledges with some embarrassment. I suppose it is easier to remain indifferent by avoiding serious investigation.

"When you read the Bible, how do you reconcile these more difficult matters?" I inquire.

"I don't," she says. Like an unresolved musical chord, she lets the tension linger. "I guess I don't see these things as that black and white. Unlike some, I am comfortable living with the gray."

I sense Katherine becoming uneasy with my line of questioning.

"There need to be more miracles," she says, attempting to lighten the mood or change the subject. "Then more of us would see for ourselves what is and isn't true."

After pointing out that Jesus took a rather dim view of those in his day who demanded miraculous signs in order to believe, I move on. Katherine looks visibly relieved that we are moving off topics she has successfully avoided in the past, and of which she hopes to steer clear in the future. She reassumes a role more suited to CEO by providing her critique of the gospel story.

"We were so stupid that we crucified Christ before giving him a chance to say all he had to say," she declares, betraying her assumption that Christ came primarily to impart a philosophy rather than pay a penalty. "I'm sure that's the way it was meant to be for some reason. But I think it would have been nicer and more beneficial to us had he been given more time to teach. It is sad that God had to send his Son into a situation where he had to be tortured and crucified to do something good for us."

As if editing a first draft document, Katherine can't seem to resist the urge to critique God's strategy for redemption. She might have managed the entire affair in a less disruptive, less painful manner. And it bugs her that people like me find Christ's sacrifice such a central, even beautiful part of the Christian message.

A Kinder, Gentler Christianity?

"I would love to find a church that presented Christianity more positively," Katherine says, attempting to summarize her lack of connection.

"How aggressively have you searched?" I again call her bluff.

"Not real aggressively." A slight smile suggests she knows her cover is blown.

"Why?"

"I don't know. I guess it just isn't comfortable for me. Something tied to my personality. I can honestly tell you I find there is no depth there. I've never been deeply moved by a sermon. I don't like to sing. I hate that. I don't like to hug my neighbor. I hate that too." She laughs, as if relieved that the game is over and she is being totally honest.

"It's all so phony! I believe in God, not church." A more defensive tone ensues, as if she is reliving a past argument, perhaps with herself. "That's probably bad. I haven't educated my children about Christianity like I should."

After explaining my passion to teach the Christian faith to my own children, I ask Katherine how she explains her laid-back approach to such a vital issue with hers. How can she raise her kids absent any religious instruction?

"I guess it is because I don't really believe non-believers go to hell."

She wonders where people find the time for church, especially when going to church seems like just another chore on the list, rather than something fun. "It's like pulling teeth. Besides, the Bible doesn't say you have to go to church."

"Why," I ask, "do you think those of us you would call 'intense' do it?"

"I have no clue." The uninhibited honesty continues. "People probably enjoy the camaraderie. Maybe I would, too, if I didn't feel it was so fake, just going through the motions."

And one thing is clear. Katherine is a *very* busy woman who can't be bothered with such nonsense.

Hard To Swallow

Christians are too intense.

Tough Questions

—The SKEPTIC—

I found God. Now it's my turn to hide.

BUMPER STICKER

CHAPTER 11

Thinking Free

"Why don't you just read the pamphlets. . . .
That will tell you what we think."

I arrived at the event about fifteen minutes early in order to do some people watching. A registration table greeted me, while the volunteer manning it did not. He remained feverishly occupied with the task of making sure plenty of name tags were available for what was shaping up to be one of the largest crowds the event had attracted in some time.

"Do I have to wear a name tag?" asked an elderly lady, a fellow first-time visitor.

"No you don't," came the volunteer's reply. "That's the great thing about being a Freethinker—you can do as you please."

It was the monthly meeting of a local Freethinkers society, a loosely organized group of atheists, agnostics, humanists, and other self-described non-believers. Loosely organized because folks attracted to such a meeting don't want anyone telling them what to think or do. As the closest thing to a creed on their website makes clear:

> Freethinkers believe in the right to freedom of belief. "Freedom of religion" includes freedom from religion. . . . Because freethinkers do not demand conformity to a bible, creed or messiah, and because freethinkers consider revelation and faith to be

invalid, we do not accept the authority of orthodoxy or self-pro-claimed dictators of morality.

It also provided some definition of who does and doesn't qualify.

What is a freethinker? A person who uses freethought to evalu-ate the likelihood that a claim is true. A freethinker depends on the quality of the evidence to reach a conclusion and is not intimidated or influenced by religious dogma or authority. A free-thinker is not constrained by tradition and is unafraid to chal-lenge unsubstantiated and unverifiable testimony, regardless of its emotional appeal.

The theater-style seats gradually fill as the crowd of folks who had been chatting in the lobby begin to leisurely stroll into the auditorium. Most sit quietly, thumbing through free literature picked up at the registration table. I grabbed some of the more interesting bits myself, including a photocopied page with a large black dot in the middle that read:

BLOW ON THIS SPOT

When it turns blue, God's promises will come true!

As expected, I'm among skeptics. Not that you would know it from observing the crowd, most of whom seem older than I anticipated. I had expected a room filled with college students, eager to defend the dogma of their favorite philosophy professor. But with few exceptions, they are senior citizens—pleasant-look-ing, gray-haired folks more suited to singing gospel hymns than mocking religious faith.

The room nearly fills to its hundred and fifty capacity; a gen-tleman in his sixties with a long, gray ponytail and neatly-groomed goatee moves to the front and greets the crowd, formally kicking off the evening. Before the speaker can be introduced, he needs to make several mundane announcements about an upcoming social and the next monthly meeting.

The big news is that the Atheist Alliance Convention is coming to town—on Easter weekend, the irony sparking spontaneous laughter and enthusiastic applause. The crowd also gets excited over recent member efforts to raise support for installing a humanist chaplain at the city hospital in order to provide an alternative for unbelieving patients and families. I wonder what words of comfort and grace such a chaplain could offer at death's door. Still, those in attendance seem encouraged by the possibility.

What happened next could have been scripted for a church comedy sketch. But it's no joke. A young student named Eric is invited to the front of the auditorium to report details of how he was "hell bent" on setting up a student-led Freethinkers club at the local high school. As he approaches the platform, the crowd cheers in celebration and appreciation for the heroic boy willing to rescue fellow students from the bondage of religious belief. I feel like I'm back in my childhood Baptist church, as older members applauded the youth group's unsophisticated but sincere evangelistic zeal, eager to sponsor their street witnessing and short-term mission projects. It feels like looking at a photographic negative of a scene repeated over and over in evangelical churches.

Eric thanks them for their encouragement and asks for their support—though he is careful to clarify that his group wants no strings attached, as they want to remain self-governed, a position he knows they would admire. "We want to create an accepting, safe place for those with alternative beliefs," Eric explains when asked about the group's goals.

"Are you going to believe or are you going to think?" comes an affirming jest from a long-time Freethinker. Eric nods with a knowing grin and completes his appeal for support. Another round of enthusiastic applause engulfs him on the trek back to his seat. I'm sure the encouragement feels good to a budding cynic seeking affirmation in his skepticism. After all, with 95 percent of the population believing in God, it must get lonely trying to take a stand for one's alternative beliefs . . . er, thoughts.

⟨∝

Announcements and affirmations out of the way, our ponytailed master of ceremonies introduces the special guest and main speaker for the evening. Kimberly is on a promotional tour for her newly released book, *The Fundamentals of Extremism*: *The Christian Right in America*. Hailing from Michigan, she is a syndicated writer with articles appearing in over a hundred publications around the country. Whether those publications include any mainstream papers is not explained, but I note that she has no academic credential in her bio.

Kimberly takes center stage. A forty-ish blond who looks a bit like country music superstar Faith Hill, she seems too thin, almost sickly—as if the book tour has taken a toll on her otherwise lovely figure. She's just the kind of spokesperson one might look for to represent your agenda: fairly attractive and seeming to have her act together.

Kimberly offers a few details of her past, including the revelation that she once called herself a Christian. As a child, her parents sent her off to Sunday school at a local fundamentalist church. They didn't go themselves, but allowed her to join friends on the church bus when it came around. Despite regular church attendance, however, Kimberly never bought the faith. "I spent ten years asking God to forgive me for not believing in him," she says, her vulnerability prompting sympathetic sighs from the crowd. "Later, I abandoned belief altogether."

To most of the audience, I'm sure this confession brings credibility to Kimberly's current fight against religious belief. After all, she had lived among the enemy. To me, however, it suggests the possibility that Kimberly is reacting against, rather than speaking for, something deep within her emotional being.

Whatever the motivation, her talk makes it clear that Kimberly has an axe to grind against what she labels "Christian Fundamentalism." It is no exaggeration or mischaracterization to say that the bottom line of her talk is that those who truly believe the Bible and Christian dogma are dangerous to society, and especially to children, African Americans, women, homosexuals, and lesbians. The evidence she offers is, to put it kindly, sophomoric. Her case would not stand the scrutiny of a high school debate coach—but this crowd eagerly receives it all.

At one point, she quotes the late Bob Jones Sr. (who has been dead nearly forty years), as evidence of the racist nature of Christian belief. As a critic of Bob Jones myself, I recognize the quotations as perhaps six decades old. But Kimberly calls them "recent" examples of lingering racism among believers.

She next references the high levels of emotional, sexual, and physical abuse among children whose parents hold conservative Christian beliefs. Of course, she offers no substantive evidence. But this crowd needs none, since her comments merely confirm something they always suspected.

One of the most bizarre accusations has something to do with a Religious Right conspiracy against Ritalin for children suffering from Attention Deficit Hyperactivity Disorder. It seems Christians are depriving children of much-needed treatment because they want more chaos in the classroom—just one more way fundamentalists are seeking to undermine and eventually destroy public schools. I have to suppress a chuckle, amazed that anyone actually believes such strange accusations.

Looking around the room, however, it is clear that many do.

ℂ

When the speaker finishes, the host invites questions and discussion from the audience while ushers pass the donation bucket. Most of the questions come from people who clearly want to hear themselves talk—much like a church Bible study. I suppose no matter where you go, those who consider themselves intellectuals dominate the discussion. But several questions come from folks who seem genuinely concerned, hoping to better understand these radical, dangerous folks called Christians.

I find myself disturbed by the kind of insidious motives being attached to Christianity. Even more troubling is the uncritical manner in which the accusations are accepted as fact. But then, I've seen the same tendency among some Christians—overly eager to repeat unsubstantiated paranoia about secular humanist plots. I guess we could all learn to listen more and talk less.

"I want to thank you for your presentation tonight," comes a compliment from a man seated in the last row who says he has read about two-thirds of Kimberly's book. "It is good to hear from someone who doesn't have a vendetta."

Had we heard the same speech?

"This is our first time at a Freethinkers gathering," Jerry says from his second-row seat next to his wife and son. "I must say it is refreshing to know there are other people like us around!" The crowd applauds warmly, as if affirming an Alcoholics Anonymous confession.

Quietly sitting through the meeting, it strikes me that there is much I do not understand or appreciate about the experience of those around me. I have my own questions. What would make someone feel so strongly about unbelief that they would spend time, energy, and in some cases money to participate in such an event? What stories might I discover behind the lives represented here? Did the speaker experience some kind of sexual abuse while attending Sunday school as a child? If I could interview each attendee, would I discover common patterns or experiences driving their skepticism?

I approach a few of the regular attendees and explain that I am working on a book about unbelief and wonder if they would be willing to chat. The first lady had helped to organize the event—quite friendly at first, eager to greet an unfamiliar face. But her smile quickly morphed into disapproval upon discovering my intentions. She literally backed away from me in panic, body language similar to that of Mike Suzinski in the movie *Monsters, Inc.*, upon encountering a real-live child invading his safe haven. A dangerous enemy had entered the camp!

I tried to calm her by explaining that I hoped to meet with one or two folks to ask questions and learn more about why they consider Christianity hard to swallow.

"Why don't you just read the pamphlets and literature back on the lobby table? That will tell you what we think."

Not exactly what I expected to hear from a freethinker. I don't know whether to laugh at the irony or keep pressing for an interview. I decide to give it one more try.

"Well, I was hoping to sit down face-to-face with someone over coffee to chat."

The tortured look on her face reminds me of a child sitting in the waiting room on immunization day, hoping the doctor never calls her name. Clearly, it would be best to ask someone less frightened by the religiously devout. "Listen, that's okay. I can tell the idea makes you nervous. I'll find someone else. Thanks anyway." The fear on her face quickly dissolves, the doctor suddenly called away.

Several more attempts reap three willing interview candidates (two, not counting the gentleman who turned out to be a Bible-believing Christian who attended with a friend as part of some sort of quid-pro-quo arrangement). Mission accomplished, I head out the door after scooping up more table literature, including several tract-like leaflets with provocative titles such as:

- Cookie Cutter Christs—Origins of the Jesus Myth
- What's Wrong with the Ten Commandments?
- Confused?—Bible Contradictions
- An X-Rated Book—Sex and Obscenity in the Bible

Each was labeled a "nontract," clearly developed in defense against the gospel tracts believers hand out on street corners or leave with waitresses instead of tips. A few excerpts from the one titled *Dear Believer* give a taste of the approach.

> *Dear Believer,*
>
> *You ask me to consider Christianity as the answer for my life. I have done that. I consider it untrue, repugnant, and harmful . . .*
>
> *If Christianity were simply untrue I would not be too concerned. Santa is untrue, but it is a harmless myth which people outgrow. But Christianity, besides being false, is also abhorrent. It amazes me that you claim to love the god of the bible, a hateful, arrogant, sexist, cruel being who can't tolerate criticism. I would not want to live in the same neighborhood with such a creature!*[1]

The nontract goes on to detail God's offenses, such as giving the command "Thou shalt not kill," and then ordering the death of all opposition, including wholesale drowning and mass exterminations, punishing the children of sinners to the fourth generation, demanding animal and human blood to appease his angry vanity, and creating hell to torture unbelievers, just to name a few. The writer also takes several pretty direct jabs at God's Son, calling him a "chip off the old block" because he claimed to be one with the Father and to uphold the Old Testament law. The beliefs of his followers, the church, don't fare much better.

> *The concepts of original sin, depravity, substitutionary forgiveness, intolerance, eternal punishment, and humble worship are all beneath the dignity of intelligent human beings and conflict with the values of kindness and reason. They are barbaric ideas for primitive cultures cowering in fear and ignorance.*[2]

If the substance of this and other nontracts reflects how most freethinkers feel about the faith I hold dear, the interview process shaped up to be a challenge. I fully expected highly emotional, confrontational rancor. To my pleasant surprise, however, I encountered a rather friendly cyborg named Ralph.

Hard To Swallow

Christianity is mindless dogma.

CHAPTER 12

Chat with a Cyborg

"We exist for the perpetuation of human DNA."

Ralph and his wife of twelve years try not to talk about religion. Her Catholicism and his "freethinking" don't mix because he considers spiritual matters a waste of time. So, for the marriage to work, they avoid the subject entirely. On this occasion, however, Ralph gladly discusses religion.

He joins me at the Village Inn restaurant without his bride or anyone else who might disagree with his description of the world, a world that excludes any sort of supernatural, a personal God, or eternal soul. A world very different from my own.

I met Ralph while attending the Freethinkers society meeting a few weeks earlier. About fifty, he is tall with a medium build, short hair, and a slight limp. An avid Trekkie, Ralph describes himself as a cyborg: part organic, part technology. His artificial hip, dental work, eyeglasses, and mobile phone all repairing or enhancing his functionality. On the surface, he seems the prototypical engineer: conservative demeanor and dress. A former military career has left its permanent imprint, even making him a right-wing conservative talk show fan.

But beneath the image, Ralph is defined and driven by a worldview so comprehensive and sophisticated that it leaves no room for Christian belief, nor patience for its childish notions. In his words, the "cost and benefit analysis" shows that a rational-

116

istic view of the world reaps a greater payback than religious adherence.

"I am a trans-humanist," Ralph begins. The look on my face suggests I don't follow. "A worthless pragmatist might be a better description. I wouldn't fit the typical humanist persona—you know, liberal tree-huggers who want to save the world while singing Kumbaya. I think most of them are totally out of touch with reality."

Ralph and his fellow trans-humanists advocate more pragmatic ideals, including the exciting innovations of technology and free-market opportunity that create "pro-social value" based upon concrete health and lifestyle improvements. He encourages me to visit a website produced by one of his philosophical heroes, containing features that highlight some of the amazing possibilities associated with current research and innovation. When I did, I discovered that a whole lot of people dream of what they consider an optimum future for us all, kind of *Brave New World* meets the Tower of Babel. Only rather than reaching for artificial happiness or heaven, they reach for artificial intelligence and synthetic life.

I quickly discover tenet one of Ralph's creed: improving the lot of humanity brings purpose and meaning to the individual life.

"We exist for the perpetuation of human DNA," he declares.

I feel a cold chill run down my spine, similar to one I got watching *Star Trek* when a passionless Mr. Spock callously explained how "the good of the many outweighs the good of the one." We are part of an impersonal machine that exists to advance the collective good. The notion feels quite disturbing for one who believes in a personal God who cares for every individual. But to Ralph and his fellow trans-humanists, this is pretty exciting stuff.

Digressing from general philosophy to more personal questions, I discover that Ralph has some knowledge of Christian theology, in part because he attended church as a child, even going through confirmation class at about age twelve to learn the fundamentals. They didn't take.

"At about age fourteen I realized, 'This just makes no sense!'" reflects Ralph.

Always curious as to whether a negative encounter with Christians has contributed to one's disbelief, I ask Ralph about his experience.

"Oh, it was all typical mainline Protestant, touchy-feely, warm stuff. There was nothing bad. Just honest, decent people. There was no untoward incident that drove me away from the church."

But he left nonetheless. Considering belief in God a silly, irrelevant notion, Ralph began calling himself an atheist at age fifteen, a word he now avoids in favor of "logical positivist." Practically speaking, there is little difference. But philosophically, it is a vital distinction allowing Ralph to avoid some of the big questions like first cause and the foundation for universal ethics. Why bother disproving the existence of God when one can take the shortcut of dismissing him?

"If you want to say that there is some process that has intelligence that causes things to progress either forward into extropy or downward into entropy, I'd say yes," Ralph concedes. "Evolutionary processes can accumulate information over time, and that's how you get extropy and a localized violation of the second law of thermal dynamics. And if people want to slap a label on it and call that process God, fine. I don't care. But if you think that process can provide hope or comfort, I say no."

Put like that, belief in God doesn't sound all that attractive to me either. Clearly, Ralph has a knack for sucking the beauty and wonder out of things.

In an effort to summarize the first tenet of Ralph's creed, I misspeak: "You don't *believe* in anything supernatural." Persnickety about word use, he corrects my description.

"No, I *think* based upon the evidence that there is no super-natural," he replies. Belief, in Ralph's lexicon, is what non-thinkers do. "Belief is irrelevant. What are the facts? What do the facts point to? What hypothesis can we derive from this? I can believe the moon is made of green cheese all day long, but it won't change the facts."

Whatever the words, however, he acknowledges that he has a basic philosophical and ethical framework, as does everyone.

Since Ralph has been part of the Freethinkers group for about a year, I ask him something that has perplexed me for weeks. "Why do people give up an evening every month to attend a Freethinkers meeting? Religious gatherings make sense to me. Even if one doesn't feel like going or care for the people, duty calls. Political gatherings also make sense, since a common agenda motivates participation. But what on earth motivates a group of folks who don't have any other reason to gather to attend such a meeting?"

"Validation of their philosophy," Ralph explains. The same rationale some would give for why Christians gather, to shore up wavering belief. Only in this case, it is to shore up unbelief. "They want to talk to others who think kind of like them, listen to authors who write about matters that are important to them."

"Such as?" I ask.

"Such as rationalism is correct. Most of the folks there are hard-core rationalists. There is so much emotionalism in the world today, and there are a lot of people making important deci-sions on an emotional basis." Ralph uses Middle East conflicts as an example. "We are tired of it! We want reason and logic to prevail." Something that can't happen as long as emotionally motivated religious belief dominates society.

Ralph's worldview allows for only that which can be grasped using the five senses. "Show me evidence for spirituality, period. It's a non-sensical word in my thought system." As a result, he explains all religious belief in terms of emotionalism. He claims to have studied most of the major world religions, including Buddhism, Hinduism, Islam, Mormonism, Catholicism, etc. So how does this rationalistic cyborg describe the essence of Christianity?

"It includes belief in a supernatural entity that can influence factors in your life. Christianity is a derivative of Judaism, which is a derivative of older, pagan beliefs from middle eastern tribes. They had these beliefs in the supernatural adopted by the Jews, modified over time from animism and tribal deities into the new idea of monotheism, belief in one God. Christianity is based upon the teachings of Christ, a Jew killed under Roman occupation in about AD 30. He had a set of principles called the Beatitudes, very firm ideas about right and wrong and some of the bureaucracy that had overtaken the Jewish religious system of that time. He was seen as a troublemaker by Jewish religious authorities because he was a threat to their power structure. They had him executed by the Romans, who didn't care one way or the other. There were certain supernatural assertions made after his death, and that has been the basis for that religion—the core belief centered around the divinity of Jesus Christ."

What things does Ralph find odd about Christianity? He lists several, including "the practice of mock cannibalism in Communion" and "the prominence of a crucifix, suggesting the entire religion is based upon somebody who was tortured to death."

"The big one," he continues, "is the dichotomy between what Christians say and what they do. Having a moral system that you only pay lip service to is kind of hokey to me. And that goes for a lot of religious beliefs, not just Christianity."

What does Ralph find offensive?

"Proselytizing from those who won't take no for an answer. Sending a missionary to my door is incredibly arrogant. I'm not an unwashed savage. I don't need your help."

What does he find attractive?

"It's warm and fuzzy emotionally. It gives a sense of belonging to a social group. And there is an intense belief and sense of security that to me is a crutch. But to them, it's their hope." Which brings us back to the Freethinkers group where I met Ralph. "Do these folks gather to attain a similar sense of hope and belonging?"

"To a lesser extent. But I don't think there's a sense of hope. In fact I think there's a sense of despair. And it is usually a lot more intellectual than the meeting you experienced." Ralph admits to feeling embarrassed at times by many fellow freethinkers because they can be sophomoric, sloppy thinkers. Most, he says, are angry women who are recovering Catholics, in rebellion against the notion that they must be baby factories. Still, he likes hanging around them, in part because it provides a forum for connection with others who share some of his ideas and interests.

But I suspect there is another reason. It gives Ralph a place to voice opinions about and arguments against Christianity he can't share at home without risking his marriage.

Is there anything dangerous about all of these irrational, emotionally driven believers running around? Or does Ralph view them as harmlessly deluded, like children believing in Santa in order to make Christmas a bit more enjoyable?

"It's a free country. People can be irrational if they want to." As long as they don't do anything to hurt others, Ralph sees it as harmless fun.

Walking through a list of specific statements associated with Christian theology, I discover that Ralph has a fairly consistent perspective. He does not believe that Jesus is God, but does see evidence that he was a historical figure who existed. On the subject of human evil, however, I encounter what seems a discrepancy in Ralph's philosophical framework. It emerges as he explains what is wrong with our world.

"There are evil people who do evil things," he says. The comment surprises me, since belief in evil can exist only in contrast to belief in objective good. I push Ralph a bit on this point, pointing out that he has made a moral judgment by calling people who harm others, "wrong." Ralph had defended a utilitarian worldview in which no absolute standards of right and wrong exist because there is no God to embody or declare them. If the fittest must harm others to survive or succeed, more power to them.

"Do you have a foundation for that moral judgment, or is it just your opinion?" I intend for my question to uncover whether Ralph is drawing upon his childhood religious training or whether he has discovered some other basis for judging one thing good and another evil.

"I'd have to think about that," he replies. "I guess a lot of it goes back to the golden rule—doing to others as you would have them do to you." A concept with a religious foundation, I point out. "I guess I don't feel a real need to go and think about a moral belief system or ethical system. I like the Golden Rule because, to me, it's honorable. And that's important to me because of my self-image and ego."

In other words, he has no real foundation for moral judgments, but is glad to make them anyway. Despite the obvious hole in his philosophy, Ralph deserves credit for intellectual honesty. He willingly concedes the inconsistency, one that grows out of lazy thinking rather than critical reflection.

Ralph has never seriously examined Christianity for himself, something I find odd considering the fact that he married a woman who has.

"I don't see a need for it," he explains. "I get by in society, am respected by my peers, and achieve well without it. I don't even need it to network because I do that on my own in other ways." Bottom line: Ralph sees no pragmatic benefit.

Does some common characteristic among believers drive them to embrace Christianity, such as being needy, or naïve, or uneducated? Why do so many people willingly accept something that, in Ralph's words, is so irrational?

"I don't know," he responds. "But I speculate that there could be a biochemical basis for it in the brain. Maybe it raises the level of serotonin to satisfy certain chemically-driven emotional needs—and those who don't believe may not experience those needs. Much like being treated for depression using drugs that help rebuild damaged pathways so that they come out happier and more euphoric. That's about the best I can do."

Ralph's explanation seems detached and dehumanizing, like a software engineer trying to explain a system glitch. In some ways, I guess that is what he is: a cyborg programmed for logic, trying to decipher the glitch of faith. He finds my view as perplexing as I find his. I consider Ralph a fairly reasonable person who can't see the obvious. He wonders why I see what plainly isn't there.

After wrapping up our conversation, Ralph and I shake hands and part company. As I get into my car, the core themes of our conversation come flooding back into my mind.

Ralph is a skeptic who sees everything through the lens of rationalistic materialism. Christianity is an irrational belief system that serves as a coping mechanism for those with emotional needs. In his world, we exist for the purpose of perpetuating our DNA—no more, no less.

As I pull away from the restaurant, I think of the dreadful implications of such a world. Another chill runs down my spine.

Hard To Swallow

Religion is a crutch for the needy.

CHAPTER 13

Oh, God!

"With your powers, you could solve so many problems.
Why don't you?"

I may find the ideas of skeptics disturbing, but that does not make them wrong. On the contrary, it actually lends credibility to their position. What sane person would settle into a world without design or purpose, unless he felt he had no viable option? Wishful thinking hardly leads to a Godless universe. That so many believe something so awful causes me to wonder why they feel trapped into the corner of disbelief.

The 1977 movie *Oh, God!* starring George Burns and John Denver, had the right idea. God took on physical form (a good-natured Burns wearing sneakers, glasses, and a sailor's cap) in order to get the attention of Larry, an agnostic grocery store manager. God is not at all what Larry expected—he cracks jokes and admits mistakes, such as making avocado pits too big—and delivers a message for the modern world.

"I exist. And I set the world up so it can work. It's up to you. You can't look to me to do it for you."

Larry, like any good skeptic, asks questions, lots of questions. His first comes in response to an intercom voice claiming to be the Almighty.

"How do I know you're God? All I hear is a voice . . ."

"You're not allowed to see me."

"Why not?"

"Because," Burns' voice counters.

"That's no answer," says an agitated, frightened Larry.

"Sue me! I don't like to brag. But if I appeared to you just as God, how I really am, what I really am, your mind couldn't grasp it."

Later in the story, while shaving in the bathroom, Larry asks a second category of questions chief in the skeptic's mind.

"With your powers, you could solve so many problems. Why don't you?" And the clearly connected, "How can you permit all the suffering that goes on in the world?"

The subject of religion is also addressed, surfacing from an inquest conducted by a panel of theologians representing major world religions.

Which of the world's religions is the closest to the divine truth?

Is Jesus Christ the Son of God?

The film portrays God as above petty details and religious preference, then concludes by poking fun at the abuses of an obnoxious, money-grubbing evangelist.

While hardly a philosophical masterpiece, *Oh, God!* successfully raises the most nagging questions of human experience.

- Why doesn't God show himself?
- Why do the innocent suffer?

It would be impossible to dive into every variation on these themes. It is enough to briefly acknowledge each as a key reason many find my faith so hard to swallow that they cannot pry their fingers loose from the scalding handle of skepticism.

An Invisible God

Why does God hide from mankind? Would it really be that hard for him to explicitly reveal himself to every person on the planet?

Couldn't he simply show up on our thirteenth birthday and explain what's what? Is that really too much to ask?

Good questions. Tough questions. Questions that motivate many skeptics to reject a foundational concept of Christian belief.

I was in my early twenties when I first began to seriously consider arguments against Christianity. While a graduate student in seminary, a few friends and I started a monthly reading group to discuss books that challenged rather than reassured our faith. One of our first selections was *The Atheist Debater's Handbook* by B. C. Johnson. We had all read famous Christian apologists offering evidence for Christianity. But we wanted to evaluate whether those arguments could withstand a direct frontal assault.

Right out of the gate, Johnson sidesteps responsibility for disproving God's existence: "The atheist, for his part, does not necessarily offer an explanation; he simply does not accept the theist's explanation. Therefore, the atheist need only demonstrate that the theist has failed to justify his position."[1]

Johnson then gives himself a distinct advantage by choosing the modern world's star player, science, as his teammate: "The theist would do well to avoid the subject of science altogether. The evidence science does provide actually contradicts traditional theism."[2]

Leaving the weak, sickly kid named "Blind Faith" for our side to choose, Johnson quickly establishes the most important rule of the game: "The atheistic position must prevail if the theist is unable to support his belief in the existence of God."[3]

In other words, unless the judge is convinced, skepticism wins. Incidentally, the judge is a skeptic.

The problem with this line of thinking, of course, is that it insists the game be played according to a flawed presupposition. The only evidence allowed into the debate is that which can be perceived with the five senses and tested in the university laboratory, thus putting believers at a distinct disadvantage. We are trying to kick the ball up an incline, only to watch it roll back toward our own unprotected goal.

Since that first encounter with one skeptic's lens, I have deciphered a similar pattern among others who insist that God must not exist because he can't be seen. Even those who spend their days peering at the complex masterpiece of creation through a microscope or telescope seem to dismiss out of hand the notion that it has an artist.

Queens' College President and Templeton Prize winner, John Polkinghorne, points out that the world is not full of items stamped "made by God" because the Creator is more subtle than that. Unfortunately, many expect him to be far more overt.[4]

I marvel that someone as bright as Carl Sagan could say with a straight face, "The cosmos is all that is, or ever was, or ever will be."

I find the words of Nobel Laureate Dr. Francis Crick oddly amusing. Observing the mind-boggling complexity of the DNA that he co-discovered, he warned, "Biologists must constantly keep in mind that what they see was not designed, but evolved."[5]

And then there is the famous skeptic Richard Dawkins, whose book satirically titled *The Blind Watchmaker* actually calls biology "the study of complicated things that give the appearance of having been designed for a purpose." This "appearance" that he later labels "apparent miracle" cannot, however, be from a designer, because that would suggest the existence of one who can't be seen. So Dawkins instead champions an explanation he admits contains "astronomical improbabilities." From his perspective, no stamped items must mean no maker.

The Bible tells us that God is a spirit. I suppose that is why he doesn't show up on our thirteenth birthdays. But it sure seems like it could save these and other skeptics a whole lot of trouble if he did.

Suffering Innocents

Even if God somehow showed his face, skeptics have an even more troubling question to pose. As John Denver's character asked George Burns, "How can you permit all the suffering that goes on in the world?"

One of the most powerful arguments ever penned against the possibility of a good God can be found in what many consider the greatest novel ever written, *The Brothers Karamazov* by Fyodor Dostoevsky. We enter the story as two of the central characters argue over the nature and existence of God.

Ivan Karamazov is making his younger brother, Alyosha, squirm by forcing him to confront one of the most challenging dilemmas facing Christian theology: How can a good God passively allow innocent little children to suffer under the cruel fist of evil?

Hardly the first or last skeptic to hang the ever-nagging problem of evil over our heads, Ivan ranks among the most effective by hitting where it hurts. He skips right past academic arguments on the generic reality of pain in an otherwise beautiful world, instead making his case with specific stories of how "the least of these" for whom Jesus claimed such affection are too often abandoned to the brutality of wicked men.

"Do you love children, Alyosha?" Ivan asks his believing sibling. "I know you love them, and you'll understand why I want to speak only of them now. If they, too, suffer terribly on earth, it is, of course, for their fathers; they are punished for their fathers who ate the apple."

Ivan's first punch: a cynical reference to the Christian doctrine of original sin. Like many familiar with the concept, he wonders how children could possibly be to blame for the misdeeds of distant ancestors. But the real squirming begins as Ivan applies this somewhat abstract idea to the concrete reality of suffering youngsters: "People speak sometimes about the 'animal' cruelty of

man, but that is terribly unjust and offensive to animals, no animal could ever be so cruel as man, so artfully, so artistically
cruel." Ivan proceeds to detail the torturous abuses man has perpetrated upon man—or more disturbingly, upon child.

> They take delight in torturing children, starting with cutting
> them out of their mother's wombs with a dagger, and ending
> with tossing nursing infants up in the air and catching them on
> their bayonets before their mothers' eyes. The main delight
> comes from doing it before their mothers' eyes.

A gentle believer who has devoted his life to alleviating physical and spiritual suffering in others, Alyosha's heart grieves such
distressing realities. If possible he, and I, would wish them out
of the world. But Ivan is just getting started.

> Imagine a nursing infant in the arms of its trembling mother,
> surrounded by Turks. They've thought up an amusing trick: they
> fondle the baby, they make it laugh, and they succeed—the baby
> laughs. At that moment a Turk aims a pistol at it, four inches
> from its face. The baby laughs gleefully, reaches out its little
> hands to grab the pistol, and suddenly the artist pulls the trigger
> right in its face and shatters its little head ... Artistic, isn't it?

Artistic, indeed. If the history of mankind reveals anything, it
tells us that we are prone to such ruthless masterpieces. The jabs
continue with one example after another, including the story of
a man with hundreds of dogs in his kennels. As Ivan tells the
tale,

> One day a house-serf, a little boy, only eight years old, threw
> a stone while he was playing and hurt the paw of the general's
> favorite hound. "Why is my favorite dog limping?" It was reported
> to him that this boy had thrown a stone at her and hurt her paw.
> "So it was you," the general looked the boy up and down. "Take
> him!" They took him, took him from his mother, and locked him
> up for the night. In the morning, at dawn, the general rode out in
> full dress for the hunt, mounted on his horse, surrounded by

spongers, dogs, handlers, huntsmen, all on horseback. The house-serfs are gathered for their edification, the guilty boy's mother in front of them all. The boy is led out of the lockup. A gloomy, cold, misty autumn day, a great day for hunting. The general orders them to undress the boy; the child is stripped naked, he shivers, he's crazy with fear, he doesn't dare make a peep ... "Drive him!" the general commands. The huntsmen shout, "Run, run!" The boy runs ... "Sic him!" screams the general and looses the whole pack of wolfhounds on him. He hunted him down before his mother's eyes, and the dogs tore the child to pieces.[6]

The obvious question need not be spoken. It is the same accusing inquiry skeptics have made since the fall of man. Why does God, the one who claims to be so good and so loving, visit such indefensible cruelty upon the innocent?

The whole world of knowledge is not worth the tears of that little child to "dear God." I'm not talking about the suffering of grown-ups, they ate the apple and to hell with them, let the devil take them all, but these little ones! ... I understand solidarity in sin among men; solidarity in retribution I also understand; but what solidarity in sin do little children have?[7]

Alyosha makes several feeble attempts to fight back. But he is clearly on the ropes, gloves held high to protect a face battered with truths too real for denial. He cannot effectively counter, per-haps overly simplistic or naïve to tangle with the most forceful blows of an unrelenting skeptic. Despite an inability to match wits with his older brother, however, Alyosha continues to believe. In fact, the end of the story shows how the younger's unwavering faith becomes the only stabilizing source of redemp-tion for a family destroyed by the fallout of a Godless worldview. Meanwhile, a once arrogant Ivan descends into insanity and eventual suicide compelled by unbelief.

I recently dozed off while reading a book as my youngest child, two-year-old Nicole, napped in her room. Uncertain how long I had been asleep, I groggily forced myself from my recliner as I heard the faint whimper of a little voice downstairs. It was not a cry of pain, but one of anxious sorrow. Watching and listening through the crack in the door, I quietly observed Nicole continue what must have been a several-minute search for any trace of family in the house.

She had never been left completely alone, and must have felt puzzled by her inability to locate Mom, Dad, or big brothers. I don't know why she missed my room, but it was clear that Nicole felt the rising panic of abandonment. By the time I shook the haze of sleep from my head, she was sitting on the floor, having a good cry. A limited vocabulary could not express what must have been going through her mind. . . .

Where is my daddy?

How could he leave me here all alone to take care of myself?

I'm scared!

Unable to endure the scene for more than a few moments, I rushed to Nicole and scooped her up into my arms to comfort and reassure. She felt relieved. So did I.

I recalled that experience while wrestling with the difficult questions posed by Ivan and other skeptics. I could not keep from running to Nicole in her brief moment of agony. Why then, I wonder, can God? How does he remain quietly concealed while his children search every room in the house for some trace of his presence? Why does he merely drop hints of his existence and concern rather than leap from behind the cracked doorway to comfort and reassure? Doesn't he know we are frightened, worried that we've been left alone to fend for ourselves in a harsh, often cruel world?

I couldn't keep myself from intervention with Nicole, even though she faced no real peril. So why does God, our supposed Father, hold back when his beloved children face mortal danger? Like Alyosha facing the skeptical Ivan, such questions make me squirm.

But then I recall something that turns the entire, troublesome encounter on its head. The ruthless attacks against the existence of a good God, given voice through the character of Ivan, were actually penned by a *believer*. The author of *The Brothers Karamazov*, Fyodor Dostoyevsky, was a member of the Orthodox Church and a man of deep, even mystical, spiritual experience. Through the words of Ivan, Dostoyevsky attacked the soft underbelly of Christianity. But the character of Alyosha revealed his ability to maintain faith when one can't answer every question.

Dostoevsky wondered why innocent children suffer. Yet he believed in a good God.

I have never seen God, or even heard his voice on an intercom. Yet I believe him there.

As I mentioned in the introduction, some of Christianity's most ardent defenders were once skeptics. Some of us find ourselves defenders and skeptics at the same time. Why then do so many feel backed into the corner of skepticism? Is their unbelief tied to the arguments made, or to something else?

Hard To Swallow

God allows suffering.

Cheap Shots

—The HECKLER—

Jesus is coming. Look busy.

BUMPER STICKER

CHAPTER 14

On Edge

> "The religions of mankind must be classed
> among the mass-delusions."

I often can't tell the difference between the pure skeptic—one who rejects the possibility of supernatural realities—and the heckler—one who has an axe to grind against believers. The same person may vacillate between the two postures.

I find the second more interesting. It has more of an edge, sort of like NHL hockey. Hecklers aren't simply trying to score points against a rival worldview; they also want to slam members of the opposing team against the glass.

I've been slammed on occasion: as one of very few Christian kids in my public high school; as the young draftsman dubbed "preacher" while working my way through seminary alongside hostile colleagues; and as the in-law who stepped in something smelly from time to time, droppings from the family's history of lapsed Catholicism. Each time I have found myself asking the same question: "What put them so on edge?"

Why are some people driven to such vitriolic attacks against Christian belief and believers? What moves them from passive doubt or simple skepticism to angry antagonism? Why can't they let it go, peacefully co-existing with those of us who are, at worst, blissfully detached from reality? After all, my church attendance and Bible reading does them no harm.

The jovial Christian heavyweight G. K. Chesterton was a prime target for rival team members to check against the glass. The problem, of course, was that they usually got hurt trying. Chesterton's massive physical size—a six-foot, four-inch frame weighing over three hundred pounds—matched his equally massive intellect. With a mind nearly as sharp as his tongue, Chesterton frequently debated some of the most famous nonbelievers of the early twentieth century, including science fiction writer H. G. Wells. His persistent encounters with unbelief during the glory years of skepticism gave him unique insight into why these people seem so on edge.

"Their criticism has taken on a curious tone;" Chesterton observed, "as of a random and illiterate heckling." Keep in mind, those he accused of "random and illiterate heckling" rank among the most articulate skeptics of his era. But rather than fear their brilliance, he tended to mock their tantrums. "Their whole atmosphere," he continues, "is the atmosphere of a reaction: sulks, perversity, petty criticism."[1]

In Chesterton's opinion, only two types of people can honestly critique Christianity: those who love it, and those who know nearly nothing about it. "The next best thing to being really inside Christianity is to be really outside it," he proposed. "The best relation to our spiritual home is to be near enough to love it. But the next best is to be far enough away not to hate it."[2] The problem, of course, is that most critics are in a third category: those raised in what they consider the cold shadow of Christian belief. For one reason or another—perhaps any of those revealed in earlier chapters of this book—they found the whole thing hard to swallow. Force a child to eat lima beans or cauliflower when he's five, and he just might hate them for life.

Setting aside the motives behind such reactions for the moment, it might be helpful to examine the fallout as expressed by a few of history's more famous hecklers—some intentionally, others as a result of achieving the status of icon among skeptics.

Christianity has been the target of what I consider unfair criticism since the days of Nero, when Christians were rumored to be cannibals and arsonists. But we need not go back that far. We begin with a man at the center of the French Enlightenment.

Voltaire

During an era in which France began to flee the religion of faith dominated by Catholicism toward a religion of reason dominated by skepticism, their escape found voice through an extremely talented and brilliant man named Francois Arouet de Voltaire—satirist, novelist, poet, dramatist, historian, and critic of Christian ideals.

Reading Voltaire is a bit like watching a sadistic child use his magnifying glass to burn the limbs off an innocent bug. He doesn't accidentally squash; he enthusiastically tortures. Voltaire so hated what he considered the irrational fanaticism of Christian belief that his anger extended to the Jews. His anti-Semitism, in contrast to that of his day, was not motivated by the idea that Jews killed Jesus, but that they had made Christianity possible. To quote Ben Redman, editor of a popular compilation of Voltaire's writings:

> He did not think of the Jews, as did so many of his contemporaries, as the murderers of Christ, or as an enduring threat to Christian children. He thought of them as the people who had made Christianity possible; as the seedbed of a religion which he despised, which he considered an affront to human intelligence ... So, when he poured out his hot lead upon the Jews ... he was really striking through them at his mortal enemy.[3]

His mortal enemy—that is what Voltaire considered the faith I hold dear. An affront to human intelligence—that is what my belief represents. Such intense hatred, it seems to me, warrants some consideration. What specific criticisms did Voltaire level against Christianity? Let's begin with his attack on sectarian religion:

> Every sect, of every kind, is a rallying point for doubt and error. . . . There are no sects in geometry. . . . When the truth is evident, it is impossible for parties and factions to arise. There has never been a dispute as to whether there is daylight at noon.[4]

Voltaire clearly despised all religions, but he considered Christianity the worst, and so made it the target of his most vicious attacks.

> I realize that you will destroy the Christ-worshipping superstition only by the arms of reason.[5]
> A wise and courageous prince, with money, troops and laws, can perfectly well govern men without the aid of religion, which was made only to deceive them; but the stupid people would soon make one for themselves, and as long as there are fools and rascals there will be religions. Ours is assuredly the most ridiculous, the most absurd and the most bloody which has ever infected the world.[6]

Voltaire reluctantly believed in a Creator, unable to imagine a watch without a watchmaker. But he felt the Christian religion needed to be wiped out "root and branch." This view extended beyond Roman Catholicism, his chief enemy, to the belief in biblical revelation, upon which the entire nonsense was built. His antagonism continued to the final moments of life when, on his deathbed, concerned priests were waved away as Voltaire snapped: "Let me die in peace!"[7]

Nietzsche

One of history's most famous skeptics, Friedrich Nietzsche, died in 1900—at the dawn of a century dominated by a worldview he helped deliver. He could be called atheism's midwife. But it might be more appropriate to call him God's abortionist.

Other than skimming a few required readings in Philosophy 101 during college, few of us have spent much time absorbing the ideas Nietzsche championed. His name may prompt a vague notion of a nineteenth-century philosopher who created a stir by declaring, "God is dead!" to the world. We might recall that he went insane toward the end of his life. But that's about it.

Some link the two recollections, suggesting that it is no accident the man who proclaimed the death of God lost his mind. Of course, the linkage may be unfair. After all, many devout believers have gone insane too. But it is interesting that Nietzsche, the man Sigmund Freud described as "the person who knew more about himself than anyone else ever had or ever would," ended up losing touch with reality. In fact, it could be argued that his "insanity" was the only sane response to the reality he affirmed. What was that reality? Again, I'll let the critic present his own case, as found in the book he considered an overview of his whole philosophy, titled *Twilight of the Idols*.

> The most general formula at the basis of every religion and morality is: "Do this and this, refrain from this and this—and you will be happy! . . . The Church and morality say: "A race, a people perishes through vice and luxury."[8]

Nietzsche opposed what he considered silly moral rules because, in his view, mankind is a mere animal driven by instinct. He mocked the religious notion that we should resist or control our desires. "The saint in whom God takes pleasure is the ideal castrate . . . Life is at an end where the 'kingdom of God' begins . . ."[9]

Not only does Christianity "castrate" real living, it manufactures a false and ferocious guilt from which we need to be released.

> The whole of the old-style psychology, the psychology of will, has as its precondition the desire of its authors, the priests at the head of the ancient communities, to create for themselves a right

to ordain punishments—or the desire to create for God a right to do so . . . Men were thought of as "free" so that they could become guilty . . . Christianity is a hang-man's metaphysics . . .[10]

Fortunately, Nietzsche offered a means of escaping the noose: "We deny God; in denying God, we deny accountability: only by doing that do we redeem the world."[11]

Unfortunately, killing God opens the door to eliminating all life made in his image, starting with those Nietzsche considered loathsome, the weak . . .

> The invalid is a parasite on society. In a certain state it is indecent to go on living. To vegetate on in cowardly dependence on physicians and medicaments after the meaning of life, the right to life, has been lost ought to entail the profound contempt of society.[12]

And ending with oneself . . . "We have no power to prevent ourselves being born: but we can rectify this error—for it is sometimes an error. When one does away with oneself one does the most estimable thing possible."[13]

As with Voltaire, Nietzsche had a particular disdain for the God of Christianity, as reflected in his book, *The Anti-Christ*:

> The Christian conception of God—God as God of the sick, God as spider, God as spirit—is one of the most corrupt conceptions of God arrived at on earth: perhaps it even represents the low water mark in the descending development of the God type . . . That the strong races of northern Europe have not repudiated the Christian God certainly reflects no credit on their talent for religion—not to speak of their taste. They ought to have felt compelled to have done away with such a sickly and decrepit product of decadence.[14]

Slam! Not content to point out disagreement or make an argument, Nietzsche seeks to insult the intelligence of those he sees as a menace to human reason.

A religion like Christianity, which is at no point in contact with actuality, which crumbles away as soon as actuality comes into its own at any point whatever, must naturally be a mortal enemy of the "wisdom of the world," that is to say of science— it will approve of all expedients by which disciplining of the intellect, clarity and severity in matters of intellectual conscience, noble coolness and freedom of intellect, can be poisoned and calumniated and brought into ill repute. "Faith" as an impera- tive is a veto against science.[15]

Finally, after a long series of similar attacks, Nietzsche moves from prosecuting attorney to sole judge of the faith I hold dear:

With that I have done and pronounce my judgment. I condemn Christianity, I bring against the Christian Church the most terrible charge any prosecutor has ever uttered ... The Christian Church has left nothing untouched by its depravity, it has made of every value a disvalue, of every truth a lie, of every kind of integrity a vileness of soul ... I call Christianity the one great curse, the one great intrinsic depravity, the one great instinct for revenge for which no expedient is sufficiently poisonous, secret, subterranean, petty—I call it the one immortal blemish of mankind ...[16]

Within one year of writing the words that revealed his under- lying life philosophy, Friedrich Nietzsche went completely mad.

Freud

Sigmund Freud gave us psychoanalysis and the super ego. He emboldened us to break free of sexual repression and to blame our parents for our problems. He legitimized a scientific disci- pline that seeks to help us cope in a sometimes crazy world through sanctuary in the professional's couch rather than the priest's confessional.

Freud, perhaps more than any other individual of the past two centuries, replaced Christianity's framework for healing the soul. Forget personal repentance and scriptural meditation; it is now prolonged therapy and childhood reflections. It makes sense, since Freud considered religion part of the problem rather than part of the solution. In his words: "The religions of mankind must be classed among the mass-delusions. No one, needless to say, who shares a delusion ever recognizes it as such."[17]

In Freud's view, mankind's religious impulse has a direct link to childhood. We yearn for the security or recall the dread of daddy. Frightened by a world without the protection and boundaries our father represented during our childhood years, we invented a replacement called God. This God provides us with the delusional comfort of believing someone is watching out for us. "When the growing individual finds that he is destined to remain a child forever, that he can never do without protection against strange superior powers, he lends those powers the features belonging to the figure of his father."[18]

The good news, of course, is that Freud found a way to transcend this childish yearning. He hoped that others would do likewise as they moved beyond ignorance and superstition. As he put it: "As the treasures of knowledge become accessible, the more widespread is the falling-away from religious belief."[19]

Although I have included his comments in this chapter, I do not consider Freud an overt heckler. While he clearly considered religious belief to be an unfortunate psychological consequence, he rarely attacked believers directly. Instead, he made us feel like naïve but relatively harmless children by admonishing us to grow up, in a manner of speaking, and give up the "fairy tales of religion" by recognizing that we have not been made in God's image, but rather we have made God in the image of our fathers.[20]

In a letter responding to a Christian offended by Freud's attacks against religious belief, Freud implied he never meant any harm. "It can be called an attack on religion in so far as any scientific investigation of religious belief presupposes disbelief. Neither in my private life nor in my writings have I ever made a secret of my being an out-and-out unbeliever."[21]

Intended or not, however, Freud's criticism and characterization of religious belief did its damage, thanks to his enormous, lingering influence.

Russell

Bertrand Russell, a prominent English atheist, compiled a series of his essays into a famous book titled *Why I Am Not A Christian*. The book summarizes his contribution to the chorus of what he considered credible objections to Christian belief. One of several high-profile skeptics whom G. K. Chesterton debated, Russell may have been at the forefront of Chesterton's thinking when describing "petty criticism" with a "curious tone."

"I am as firmly convinced that religions do harm," proclaimed Russell, "as I am that they are untrue." He questioned the very existence of the God Christians worship. In his view, such belief merely perpetuated a notion gleaned in childhood. "Most people believe in God because they have been taught from early infancy to do it, and that is the main reason."[22]

More than childish, theism rests upon a crumbling intellectual foundation.

> The arguments that are used for the existence of God change their character as time goes on. They were at first hard intellectual arguments embodying certain quite definite fallacies. As we come to modern times they become less respectable intellectually and more and more affected by a kind of moralizing vagueness.[23]

Unlike Voltaire, Russell rejected the idea of a Creator as "first cause." He saw the argument that a watch cannot make itself unsatisfactory since, in his view, one still has to explain the watchmaker. "If everything must have a first cause, then God must have a cause. If there can be anything without a cause, it may just as well be the world as God, so that there cannot be any validity in that argument."[24]

Despite the fact that, in Russell's view, Christ could not have been divine, he did admire some of Jesus' teachings.

> I think that there are a good many points upon which I agree with Christ a great deal more than the professing Christians do. I do not know that I could go with Him all the way, but I could go with Him much further than most professing Christians can ... He says "If thou wilt be perfect, go and sell that which thou hast, and give to the poor." That is a very excellent maxim, but, as I say, it is not much practiced. All these, I think, are good maxims, although they are a little difficult to live up to. I do not profess to live up to them myself; but then, after all, it is not quite the same thing as for the Christian.[25]

Admiring some of his ideas, however, did not keep Russell from condemning Jesus as ultimately immoral and inhumane. "There is one very serious defect to my mind in Christ's moral character, and that is that He believed in hell. I do not myself feel that any person who is really profoundly humane can believe in everlasting punishment."[26]

Russell pointed to the incident when Jesus condemned a fig tree for failing to bear fruit as yet another reason he couldn't rank among the best teachers.

> This is a very curious story, because it was not the right time of year for figs, and you really could not blame the tree. I cannot myself feel that either in the matter of wisdom or in the matter of virtue Christ stands quite as high as some other people known to history. I think I should put Buddha and Socrates above Him in those respects.[27]

And the religion Christ inspired ranks even lower than its founder. "I say quite deliberately that the Christian religion, as organized in its churches, has been and still is the principal enemy of moral progress in the world."[28]

I find it interesting that Russell, one of the most prominent unbelievers of any day, offered what seem rather flimsy arguments. Case in point, his effort to blame God for human evil.

If I were going to beget a child knowing that the child was going to be a homicidal maniac, I should be responsible for his crimes. If God knew in advance the sins of which man would be guilty, He was clearly responsible for all the consequences of those sins when He decided to create man. The usual Christian argument is that the suffering in the world is a purification for sin and is therefore a good thing. This argument is, of course, only a rationalization of sadism; but in any case it is a very poor argument. I would invite any Christian to accompany me to the children's ward of a hospital, to watch the suffering that is there being endured, and then to persist in the assertion that those children are so morally abandoned as to deserve what they are suffering. In order to bring himself to say this, a man must destroy in himself all feelings of mercy and compassion. He must, in short, make himself as cruel as the God in whom he believes.[29]

You'd be hard pressed to find a Christian theologian who considers suffering in our world good because it purifies the soul. Yes, God uses suffering in our lives. But all evil, including human suffering, can be traced to angelic and human rebellion. When we rejected the good God is, we were left with the evil he isn't. I must agree with Chesterton that such arguments sound like "random and illiterate heckling."

Russell joined many fellow critics with one final slam, replacing the historic explanation for evil with a new, sinister culprit.

It would seem, therefore, that the three human impulses embodied in religion are fear, conceit, and hatred. The purpose of religion, one may say, is to give an air of respectability to these passions, provided they run in certain channels. It is because these passions make, on the whole, for human misery that religion is a force for evil . . .[30]

Faith of the Fatherless

New York University professor of psychology Paul Vitz offers an intriguing explanation for the "curious tone" Chesterton sensed among these and other hecklers. While Freud and others described Christian belief as an attempt to meet emotional attachment needs left over from childhood, Vitz suggests just the opposite. In his book *Faith of the Fatherless*, he makes a case for atheism as one consequence of an unhealthy or absent relationship with dear old dad. That is at least part of what's behind the seeming irrational venom of heckling unbelief.

"I am quite convinced," Vitz offers in an effort to explain what might motivate the attacks, "that for every person strongly swayed by rational argument, there are countless others more affected by nonrational, psychological factors . . . I propose, then, that irrational, often neurotic, psychological barriers to belief in God are of great importance."[31]

Vitz examines the actual childhood experience of some of history's most famous atheists, including Voltaire, Neitzsche, Freud, and Russell. All of them had a poor relationship or no relationship with their fathers, a sharp contrast to the relatively healthy relationships found between those on the other end of faith's spectrum, such as Blaise Pascal, Søren Kierkegaard, even G. K. Chesterton.

He concludes that there is a psychological aspect to unbelief, particularly when expressed as the kind of heckling we've explored in this chapter. Of course, this is not the whole story. After all, for every fatherless atheist who attacks Christianity, there are believers who find solace in the fatherhood of God despite an abusive parent. Still, we cannot ignore the influence of painful experiences on one's belief system. For better or worse, what happens to us seems to trigger something in us. Sometimes it surfaces as vitriolic attack. But, as we will discover in the next chapter, it can also come wrapped in a wisecrack.

Hard to Swallow
Christianity seems childishly naïve.

CHAPTER 15

Nervous Laughter

"My father takes after his Aunt May. She rejected the Bible
because it had an unbelievable central character."

I remember the first time I saw a Christian fish logo on the back
of a car. Impressed by the connection to a secret symbol of the
early church, I thought, *Now, that's cool.*

Years later I saw the same logo with feet on the bottom and
the name "Darwin" in the middle. Struck by the clever irony, I
remember thinking, *Now, that's funny!*

I suppose I should have felt offended rather than tickled.
Someone, somewhere created that logo in an effort to slam Christians against the glass—a person who probably takes his or her
unbelief way too seriously. I'm sure my laughing missed the
intent.

But other believers felt the insult, even going so far as to
launch a counterattack on their bumpers by displaying a reduced
Darwin fish being eaten by a larger Christian fish in "survival
of the fittest" manner. Not quite as original—kind of like kids
shouting, "Same to you and more of it!"—but a worthy effort,
nonetheless.

Do you remember the awkward thrill of that first dirty word
uttered with your grade-school friends? Knowing it was wrong
made it worth doing. The risk of being caught made it exciting.
Both prompted anxious laughter.

Satire, unlike other forms of heckling, has such an effect because it does not have to play fair. The whole point is to create an exaggerated caricature that misrepresents or overstates. When debating, both sides must be given equal time and voice. In satire, one side has a good snicker at the other's expense. Sometimes, it is a nervous laugh, as in Monty Python's 1979 release, *Life of Brian.*

The film opens with a musical score reminiscent of biblical epics such as *Ben Hur* or *King of Kings,* angelic voices serenading the silhouette of three camel-riding wise men following a star into the city of Bethlehem. They find a stable with a young mother whose infant child lies in a straw-filled manger among the animals. As they attempt to offer gifts of gold, frankincense, and myrrh, the wise men get verbally accosted by the woman they have frightened with their annoying intrusion. It is not the blessed virgin, mother of Jesus, the holy Son of God. It is squealing Monty Python star Terry Jones, portraying a promiscuous woman, mother of Brian—bastard son of a Roman guard. Quickly realizing the mistake, the wise men retrieve their gifts and scurry off to worship the true object of their quest, just next door.

Born on the same day in the next stable, the rest of Brian's life similarly parallels that of Jesus, including some fringe encounters between the two. One of the funniest scenes has Brian and others listening to Jesus' famous Sermon on the Mount from the back of the crowd. But they are so far away it is a strain to hear properly.

"Speak up!" shouts Brian's agitated mother. "I can't hear a thing!" Neither, it seems, can the others.

"What was that?" asks a nobleman who didn't quite catch Jesus' last phrase.

"I think it was, 'Blessed are the cheese makers,'" offers a fellow bystander.

"What's so special about cheese makers?" someone asks with a sigh.

"Well, obviously it's not meant to be taken literally," responds the nobleman in smug confidence of his interpretative skills. "It refers to any manufacturer of dairy products."

Similar misunderstandings and misinterpretations abound, including the assumption that some Greek is going to inherit the earth. "Did anyone catch his name?" asks one hoping to join the windfall.

In another scene, Brian encounters an unusual beggar. Perfectly healthy, he sits on the side of the road with cup extended, shouting, "Alms for an ex-leper?" Upon inquiry, Brian learns that the man was a victim of Jesus' healing powers.

"One minute I'm a leper with a trade, the next minute my livelihood is gone. Bloody do-gooder!" sneers the healed man. Apparently, miracles mess up the way things are meant to be. People should leave well enough alone.

Later, while running from the authorities, who want him arrested for involvement with a group of incompetent insurgents, Brian finds himself in a tight spot. He pretends to be a traveling preacher. A small crowd gathers to listen, but Brian loses his train of thought in mid-sentence.

"To them only shall be given . . ."

"Shall be given what?" asks the crowd.

"Oh, nothing"—an honest reply, but not good enough for his self-appointed disciples. So they fill in the blanks, each presumption building on the last.

"It must be a secret."

"What is the secret?"

"What is the secret of eternal life?"

"I want to know the secret of eternal life!"

"Tell us, master!"

Before he knows what has happened, a mass of people follow Brian, clinging to (though misunderstanding) his every word and cradling his dropped sandal as a religious relic. He attempts to correct their impressions, but can't dissuade their erroneous speculation about his mission and the meaning of his "example."

While hiding from the crowd in hopes of fleeing their adoration, Brian steps on the foot of an old hermit who has maintained a vow of strict silence for eighteen years, causing the man to scream in pain. When the crowd learns that Brian has "healed" one who had been speechless, it only fuels their zealous conjecture that he is the true messiah.

"I'm not the messiah!" insists an exasperated Brian.

"I say you are, Lord," retorts one disciple. "And I should know. I've followed a few."

In the end, Brian finds himself dying on a cross as part of a group hanging, as his fellow conspirators pay respects by reading a formal referendum honoring Brian for staying true to the point of martyrdom. They even sing him a robust round of, "For he's a jolly good fellow!" in celebration of his sacrificial example for the cause.

Film credits roll as a joyful, ever optimistic chap hanging alongside Brian encourages him to cheer up and find the silver lining of the situation, even leading the choir of condemned men in a whistling, pick-me-up tune called "Always look on the bright side of life."

Life of Brian has much of the nonsensical silliness and irreverent dialogue made legendary by the Monty Python team. But something deeper is at work in its creative choices. The movie consistently hints at the discredited, yet lingering arguments against Christ's divinity, portraying Brian as one who could just as easily have been assumed the Messiah by the uneducated, overly eager peasants of his day. Anyone who has studied the standard explanations of liberal theologians will recognize the themes:

• Jesus was the illegitimate son of a Roman guard.

- Jesus did not perform miracles; that would mess up the God-ordained order of things. His followers saw what they wanted to see.
- Jesus was a good teacher, but he never claimed to be Messiah. Disciples read that idea into his words, hearing what they wanted to hear.
- Jesus' crucifixion was not part of some divine plan to save mankind, but an injustice orchestrated by those whose power structure was threatened by his popularity.
- Jesus did not rise from the dead. His disciples stole the body in order to put a happy face on an otherwise tragic ending.

Is *Life of Brian* a funny movie? At times. Is it innocent fun? I don't think so. It is at best a commentary on just how naïve and fanatical mankind can be when it comes to religious faith. It is at worst a direct slam against the divinity of Christ. Either way, I place its humor in the category of laughter that must have accompanied creation of Darwin fish logos and other sacrilegious satire, famously demonstrated in the comedy of two American icons: nineteenth-century writer Mark Twain and twentieth-century director Woody Allen.

Mark Twain

Once the most famous American writer in the world, Mark Twain mastered ironic humor with a cynical twist. Propelled to infamy by his stories featuring Tom Sawyer and a mischievous misfit named Huck Finn, Twain offered a distinctive voice among the giants of his day—including Charles Dickens, Leo Tolstoy, Victor Hugo, and Fyodor Dostoyevsky. While these and other literary masters confronted social ills, Mark Twain poked fun at social quirks, the most glaring being the simplistic faith of his fellow Americans.

Twain's subtle jabs at Christianity surface throughout many of his books, mostly as naïve conversations between or reflections of his most loveable characters. One of my favorites is when Huckleberry Finn tries to sort out the point of praying.

> Then Miss Watson she took me in the closet and prayed, but nothing come of it. She told me to pray every day, and whatever I asked for I would get it. I tried it. Once I got a fish-line, but no hooks. It warn't any good to me without hooks. I tried for the hooks three or four times, but somehow I couldn't make it work. By and by, one day, I asked Miss Watson to try for me, but she said I was a fool. She never told me why, and I couldn't make it out no way.
>
> I sat down, one time, back in the woods, and had a long think about it. I says to myself, if a body can get anything they pray for, why don't Deacon Winn get back the money he lost on pork? Why can't the widow get back her silver snuffbox that was stole? Why can't Miss Watson fat up? No, says I to myself, there ain't nothing in it.[1]

Twain's books are filled with similarly playful satire. Below the surface, however, lurked a much darker contempt, revealing itself more plainly in later writings.

For several decades after his death, Mark Twain's daughter, Clara Clemens, resisted the release of her father's short book titled *Letters from the Earth*. Once published, the reason for her apprehension became clear. The book sheds light on a side of her father better left in the shadows of obscurity. It revealed a bitter, deeply cynical man eager to spew venom at the God of Christianity.

The book presents a series of letters written by Lucifer to his angelic colleagues, Michael and Gabriel. Lucifer is not a fallen rebel, but an angel in good standing who visits the earth many generations after the Creator wound our world's clock and left it to its own devices. Lucifer sends back reports of how the odd inhabitants of this little planet have evolved, including the imag-

inative religion they have concocted. In his first letter, for example, Lucifer describes what he has discovered:

> Moreover—if I may put another strain upon you—he thinks
> he is the Creator's pet. He believes the Creator is proud of him;
> he even believes the Creator loves him; has a passion for him;
> sits up nights to admire him; yes, and watch over him and keep
> him out of trouble. He prays to Him, and thinks He listens. Isn't
> it a quaint idea? . . . I must put one more strain upon you: he
> thinks he is going to heaven! . . . He has salaried teachers who
> tell him that. They also tell him there is a hell, of everlasting fire,
> and that he will go to it if he doesn't keep the Commandments.[2]

Lucifer goes on to describe the heaven we've imagined—
where we will spend forever doing what we don't like, such as
singing and playing harps—and where what we most like, sexual intercourse, doesn't exist. But Twain's most toxic attacks surface as Lucifer tries to explain the Commandments our "salaried
teachers" have invented for us to obey.

> He says, naïvely, outspokenly, and without suggestion of
> embarrassment: "I the Lord thy God am a jealous God." You see,
> it is only another way of saying, "I the Lord thy God am a small
> God; a small God, and fretful about small things." He was giv-
> ing a warning: he could not bear the thought of any other God
> getting some of the Sunday compliments of this comical little
> human race—he wanted all of them for himself.[3]

Later, he turns yet another command on its head, using it as
a weapon against the law-giver himself.

> According to the belief of these people, it was God himself
> who said: "Thou shalt not kill." It is plain that he cannot keep
> his own commandments.[4]

This passage is particularly telling when you learn that Twain
wrote *Letters from the Earth* after the death of a child he considered the apple of his eye. She became ill during a world speaking

tour forced upon him by financial ruin. He hated speaking tours, but debts mounted and he needed the cash. Twain received word of his daughter's illness while he was thousands of miles from America. He wanted desperately to comfort and nurture his precious girl, but could not reach home in time. She died, and they lowered her cold body into the ground while a grieving Twain grudgingly peddled his celebrated wit to the highest-paying audiences.

Even though Twain was surrounded by devout Christian believers—or maybe because of it—he pulled no punches when it came to their object of faith, Jesus Christ. He didn't buy the image of a God kinder and gentler than the harsh, Old Testament law-giver. If anything, Jesus made things worse. As Twain's Lucifer explains:

> Now here is a curious thing. It is believed by everybody that while he was in heaven he was stern, hard, resentful, jealous, and cruel; but that when he came down to earth and assumed the name Jesus Christ, he became the opposite of what he was before: that is to say, he became sweet, and gentle, merciful, forgiving, and all harshness disappeared from his nature and a deep and yearning love for his poor human children took its place. Whereas it was as Jesus Christ that he devised hell and proclaimed it!
>
> Which is to say, that as the meek and gentle Savior he was a thousand billion times crueler than ever he was in the Old Testament—oh, comparably more atrocious than ever he was when he was at his very worst in those old days![5]

Lucifer concludes Twain's heckling by declaring the God of Christianity a conscienceless, moral bankrupt. After all, he reflects, the same being who as Jesus gave us the poetic Beatitudes also joyfully ordered the slaughter of countless Midianite women and children as the God of Israel. "The Beatitudes and the quoted chapters from Numbers and Deuteronomy ought always to be read from the pulpit together";

Twain suggests, "then the congregation would get an all-round view of Our Father in Heaven."[6]

Woody Allen

I consider the life of actor, writer, and director Woody Allen irrefutable proof that God has a sense of humor. If his deer-in-the-headlights, horn-rimmed-glasses eyes, and paranoid pip-squeak demeanor don't cause one to laugh, his brilliant screenplays will. And I do mean brilliant. Allen has to be one of the sharpest minds ever to bring comedy to the silver screen.

From his Academy Award–winning *Annie Hall*, to the futuristic satire *Sleeper*, to his parody of Dostoevsky's *Crime and Punishment*, Allen has demonstrated an uncanny capacity for finding humor in the most unlikely places. Not the shallow, slapstick humor of most Hollywood fare, but a dark, nihilistic humor of one tormented by the inability to believe.

I will never forget the first time I saw one of Allen's lesser known, lesser understood films titled *Love and Death*—a faint reflection of Tolstoy's classic *War and Peace*. Other than that Allen plays a Russian farmer caught up in the dramatic events of Napoleon's Europe, the two tales bear little resemblance. Allen plays Boris Grushenko, a cowardly embarrassment to his family, but a man in love with his beautiful cousin, Sonya, played by Allen's usual sidekick, Diane Keaton.

In an opening scene, Boris and Sonya have a remarkably profound conversation for what many might consider a simple comedy, a conversation that reveals Allen's depth as a writer.

SONJA: Boris, look at this leaf. Isn't it perfect? Ah, yes. I definitely think that this is the best of all possible worlds.

Boris shrugs in disinterest and makes a wise crack
about it being the most expensive world.

SONJA: Isn't nature incredible!

BORIS: To me nature is spiders and bugs and big fish eating little
        fish, and animals eating other animals. It's like an
        enormous restaurant. That's the way I see it.

SONJA: Yes, but if God created it, it has to be beautiful, even if his
        plan's not apparent to us at the moment.

*With a roll of his eyes, Boris reveals impatient contempt with
the silly beliefs of his lovely, if unsophisticated, cousin.*

BORIS: Sonja, what if there is no God?

Sonja responds in shocked indignation as Boris continues.

BORIS: What if we're just a bunch of absurd people who are
        running around with no rhyme or reason?

SONJA: But if there is no God, then life has no meaning. Why go
        on living? Why not just commit suicide?

BORIS: Well, let's not get hysterical! I could be wrong. I'd hate
        to blow my brains out and then read in the papers they
        found something.

*Nervous laugh number one. Suddenly, the seemingly naïve
Sonja becomes an intellectual force to reckon with as the two
trade philosophical arguments for and against God.*

SONJA: Boris, let me show you how absurd your position is.
        Let's say that there is no God and each man is free to
        do exactly as he chooses. Well, what prevents you from
        murdering someone?

BORIS: Murder is immoral.

SONJA: Immorality is subjective.

BORIS: Yes, but subjectivity is objective.

SONJA: Not in any rational scheme of perception.

BORIS: Perception is irrational. It implies immanence.

SONJA: But judgment of any system or *a priori* relation of
        phenomena exists in any rational or metaphysical or
        at least epistemological contradiction to an abstract an
        empirical concept such as "being" or "to be" or "to occur
        in the thing itself" or "of the thing itself."

BORIS: Yea, I've said that many times.

Even those who don't "get the joke" buried in such lofty language, sense nervous laugh number two. When pushed to the wall with real arguments for the existence of an ultimate reality called God, Allen's character has but one response: a well-timed wisecrack.

SONJA: We must believe in God.

BORIS: If I could just see one miracle—a burning bush, or the seas part, or my Uncle Sasha pick up a check!

And with that, the conversation ends. But not before revealing an undercurrent of nihilistic angst that has surfaced throughout Woody Allen's creative career. The question of God's existence finds its way into most of Allen's films, and the answer is generally accompanied by the kind of paranoid humor we've come to associate with Allen. Here are a few such gems:

From Stardust Memories:

"To you—to you I'm an atheist . . . to God I'm the loyal opposition."

From Monologue:

"I was in love my freshman year but I did not marry the first girl I fell in love with because there was a tremendous religious conflict at the time. She was an atheist and I was an agnostic. We didn't know which religion not to bring the children up in."

From Broadway Danny Rose:

DANNY: It's very important to be guilty. I'm guilty all the time and I never did anything. You know? My rabbi, Rabbi Perlstein, used to say we're all guilty in the eyes of God.

TINA: You believe in God?

DANNY: No, no. But, uh, I'm guilty over it.

And one of my favorites, from *Crimes and Misdemeanors*:

"My father takes after his Aunt May. She rejected the Bible because it had an unbelievable central character."[7]

What I find most interesting about Woody Allen is his grasp of the arguments for belief. At times he seems more familiar with Jewish and Christian theology than many die-hard believers. How else could he write screenplays in which characters argue both sides of the God debate? And yet, despite brief beams of light that a good sense of humor can't help but reflect, his works possess an omnipresent shadow of despair. So we laugh, but nervously.

Perhaps the spirit of this heckler is best captured in a piece by Allen titled "My Philosophy." Ever the humorist, he summarizes his entire life philosophy in one brief sentence, tapping the deep wells of atheism and nihilism that have darkened his artistic expression for three decades.

Not only is there no God, but try getting a plumber on weekends.

I suppose that says it all.

Hard to Swallow

Christianity makes us nervous.

Hard Sayings

—The UNEASY—

Come the Rapture,
can I have your car?

BUMPER STICKER

CHAPTER 16

I Wish He Hadn't Said That

"Whoever believes in him is not condemned,
but whoever does not believe stands condemned already."

Believers don't need skeptics or hecklers to point out the un-pleasant or embarrassing aspects of our faith. The Bible itself does a pretty good job of keeping us off balance. In fact, on more than one occasion I have found myself wishing Jesus had held his tongue. Don't get me wrong; I believe and trust his words with all of my being. But they still make me cringe from time to time.

Apparently, I'm not alone. A number of deeply committed Christians admit that certain portions of Scripture make them uneasy. I suppose that's why we rarely mention the harder say-ings, gravitating to the more pleasant passages—like the gentle shepherd of Psalms or "the greatest of these is love" from First Corinthians.

God would have a very different image had he let me describe him to the human race. I would have presented him as nicer, less prone to wrath, and more willing to overlook offense. I would have done a better job concealing aspects of his character that many consider disagreeable. I suppose that is why he wrote his own book and why he revealed himself in the first person through the incarnation. God didn't want to be promoted and sold. He wanted to be known.

One of the reasons I believe in the God of the Bible is that he is much more than I want him to be—someone to fear, not just fancy; someone willing to redeem but entitled to condemn. Someone who said things I wish he hadn't. I can't imagine God as human invention, since in our desire to make him better, we would have made him less.

During several interviews with unbelievers, I stumbled onto a surprising discovery. They have the impression that believers enthusiastically and unreservedly accept every difficult concept found in the Bible, welcoming truths any thinking or compassionate person would reject out of hand. I guess we do a pretty good job wearing our salesman faces, since most seemed surprised to learn that many devout Christians, myself included, struggle with the harder sayings of Scripture. The fact that we believe them does not mean we like them, or even fully understand them. Let's take a look at a few biblical sayings that cause many of us to cringe.

"By the Seventh Day God Had Finished . . ."

Once upon a time, the idea that God created the world and all living creatures in less than a week seemed reasonable. After all, if an all-powerful being decided to whip up the cosmos, why dilly dally? It made perfect sense.

Then an alternative theory came along, suggesting that gradual changes over long periods of time had formed the diverse and complex world we inhabit. And that cast the Genesis creation account in a bad light:

> God saw all that he had made, and it was very good. And there was evening, and there was morning—the sixth day. Thus the heavens and the earth were completed in all their vast array. By the seventh day God had finished the work he

*had been doing; so on the seventh day he rested from all his
work. (Genesis 1:31–2:3)*

How could a process thought to require billions of years be
completed in six twenty-four-hour days? The question spawned
tension between the competing orthodoxies of science and religion that has lasted more than a century. It also prompts believers to turn an embarrassed shade of red during biology class in
school or when reading the latest find of paleontologists. Sure,
recent debates over intelligent design have boosted the waning
confidence of long-defensive believers. But we still squirm that
our biblical account of creation seems to leave little room for
incorporating apparently solid scientific discoveries.

"Sin Is Crouching at Your Door"

In the world's first incidence of sibling rivalry, a nice kid named
Abel gets killed during his jealous brother's temper tantrum. A
tragedy, for sure. But something even more disturbing surfaces
when we learn what triggered Cain's wrath.

> *Now Abel kept flocks, and Cain worked the soil. In the
> course of time Cain brought some of the fruits of the soil
> as an offering to the LORD. (Genesis 4:2–3)*

So far, so good. Cain seeks to honor God with a portion of his
bounty. Abel does likewise, offering the finest of his flock. Two
good religious kids trying their best to worship the Lord as best
they know how.

> *The LORD looked with favor on Abel and his offering, but on
> Cain and his offering he did not look with favor. So Cain was
> very angry, and his face was downcast. (Genesis 4:4–5)*

Can you blame him? Like a child holding up his best Crayola
masterpiece, Cain must have anticipated daddy's smiling
approval. Instead, he received a frown.

> *Then the* LORD *said to Cain, "Why are you angry? Why is*
> *your face downcast? If you do what is right, will you not be*
> *accepted? But if you do not do what is right, sin is crouching*
> *at your door." (Genesis 4:6–7)*

We know the rest of the story. A dejected Cain lures younger brother into an open field to take his life. If you can't color the best picture, eliminate the competition.

While we rightfully condemn Cain for murder, we also wonder why a God known as a loving Father rejected his child's well-intentioned offering. Wouldn't it be better if he accepted folks like Cain, even when they fail to meet his seemingly arbitrary criteria for proper worship? This passage seems to suggest that he is too persnickety for such approval—harshly condemning every sincerely expressed religion caught coloring outside the lines.

"Now Kill All the Boys"

Another biblical story that suggests our loving heavenly Father might have a dark side appears in the book of Numbers when the Lord orders Moses to take vengeance on the Midianites for long-ago offenses against Israel. Characteristic of much Old Testament Scripture, the story reflects an "eye for an eye" philosophy more than a "turn the other cheek" approach in its response to mistreatment.

> *They fought against Midian, as the* LORD *commanded*
> *Moses, and killed every man . . . The Israelites captured the*
> *Midianite women and children and took all the Midianite*
> *herds, flocks and goods as plunder. They burned all the*
> *towns where the Midianites had settled, as well as all their*
> *camps. They took all the plunder and spoils, including the*
> *people and animals . . . (Numbers 31:7–11)*

Harsh? It certainly seems like it. But war is hell, and we expect soldiers to overdo it when conquering enemy territory. At least they protected women and children in compliance with the guidelines of just war. Moses shouldn't be too upset with his soldiers.

In the next scene, however, Moses becomes quite angry—not because they were too harsh, but because they were too gentle.

> *Moses was angry with the officers of the army . . . "Have you allowed all the women to live?" he asked them. "They were the ones who followed Balaam's advice and were the means of turning the Israelites away from the* LORD *in what happened at Peor, so that a plague struck the* LORD's *people. Now kill all the boys. And kill every woman who has slept with a man, but save for yourselves every girl who has never slept with a man." (Numbers 31:14–18)*

The Israeli army is ordered to slaughter civilian women and children. So much for just war guidelines! One can only imagine the bloodbath Moses' order ensued—pregnant girls and frightened little boys dying at the tip of a sword.

How do we reconcile this scene with the teachings of Jesus about loving our enemies and forgiving those who trespass against us? It is difficult—which is why I list it among the portions of Scripture I wish could be ignored.

"Whoever Does Not Believe Stands Condemned Already . . ."

I understand why God would condemn Joseph Stalin or Adolf Hitler. Their willful defiance and crimes against humanity place them clearly in the "doomed" category. What is harder to accept, however, is universal condemnation as described by Jesus just after his beloved, "For God so loved the world" comments of John 3:16.

Whoever believes in him is not condemned, but whoever does
not believe stands condemned already because he has not
believed in the name of God's one and only Son. (John 3:18)

Why didn't God program the system to work in our favor?
Rather than default to eternal life, why did he set it to condemnation? To be forgiven one must believe. For damnation, however, no action is required.

"But none are innocent," we might argue. "After all, Romans
3:23 tells us that all have sinned and fallen short of the glory of
God."

Fine. So nobody is perfect. Does that mean all must be condemned? Why must the path to destruction be "wide" with many entering, while the road to life so "narrow" that few can find it (Matthew 7:13–14)? On the surface of things, the whole system seems backward to us.

"Whoever Eats My Flesh and Drinks My Blood Has Eternal Life"

Early Christians were accused of cannibalism because they were reported to eat flesh and drink blood. A mistaken impression or a logical assumption based upon Jesus' words? You decide.

Jesus said to them, "I tell you the truth, unless you eat the
flesh of the Son of Man and drink his blood, you have no
life in you. Whoever eats my flesh and drinks my blood has
eternal life, and I will raise him up at the last day. For my
flesh is real food and my blood is real drink. Whoever eats
my flesh and drinks my blood remains in me, and I in him."
(John 6:53–54)

Many who heard Jesus firsthand found this concept so offensive they stopped following him. They did not assume the flesh and blood merely symbolic of some spiritual truth. They took them literally.

> On hearing these words, many of his disciples said, "This is a hard teaching. Who can accept it?" (John 6:60)

A good question. True followers of Jesus throughout history have wrestled with these words. Some accept them as the mysterious reality Christ suggests—eating and drinking the Eucharist to receive his offer of salvation into our very being. Others take communion as a merely symbolic reminder of Christ's death on the cross, a way of celebrating our healing through his suffering.

Whether or not one accepts the elements as the literal body and blood of Christ, practicing the Lord's Supper continues to be a distinguishing mark of Christian faith because it is the means whereby we proclaim that his death redeems our life. And no matter how precious Jesus' words about eating his body and drinking his blood may be to those of us who believe, they remain a mysteriously hard teaching.

"No One Comes to the Father Except through Me"

They may be the most disturbing two sentences Jesus uttered during his earthly ministry—nineteen words confronting us with a clear choice.

> "I am the way and the truth and the life. No one comes to the Father except through me." (John 14:6)

There is no mistaking his meaning. Jesus did not leave us the option of viewing every sincere religious pursuit as equally valid. He did not offer himself as one path among many to the same destination. Jesus described himself as the only way to God; end of story. Various world religions are not alternative routes. They are at best rabbit trails, at worst roads to hell paved with good intentions.

It is no exaggeration to place these two sentences among the most troubling tenets of Christian belief. Frankly, I sometimes wish we could hold a less exclusive view. It would be nice to view Jesus as one among many mystics, prophets, or avatars pointing us to God. I wish Cain's offering was as acceptable as Abel's. I would like to believe that Jews, Muslims, Mormons, Hindus, and Buddhists are all saying the same thing with different words. But Jesus did not leave that option, no matter how much I might wish he had.

"He Must Deny Himself and Take Up His Cross and Follow Me"

I recall a comment by Sarah, one of the dabblers from chapter 4, who said she liked the idea of God because it would bring comfort. Apparently, she hasn't heard one of Jesus' more unsettling declarations.

> Then he called the crowd to him along with his disciples and said: "If anyone would come after me, he must deny himself and take up his cross and follow me. For whoever wants to save his life will lose it, but whoever loses his life for me and for the gospel will save it." (Mark 8:34–35)

To be blunt, I wish Jesus hadn't said that. It disturbs Sarah's ideal of the warm, peaceful feelings associated with religious belief. You know the image: troubled folks escaping the harsh realities of life by believing in a loving God who leads us beside the still waters and protects us through the valley of the shadow of death. Jesus' words instead suggest a God who shoves our face in the rapids of life while we struggle for air.

"If you want to live," comes the call of Christ, "give up your life!"

Not exactly the best marketing campaign if you hope to attract new converts. Not exactly the kind of religious comfort Sarah and others admire.

Christianity is anything but an escape to a pleasant stroll down easy street. It is an invitation to follow Jesus—one who bore a cross and gave his life for others. And no matter how unsettling it may seem, he expects the same from us.

"God Chose the Foolish . . ."

I like to think of myself as a reasonably intelligent person. I want to be perceived as perceptive and well read, a smarter-than-average-age guy who deserves the respect of the educated class. I listen to National Public Radio, watch the Discovery Channel on television, and rarely take tabloid headlines seriously. I see my Christian beliefs as reasonable, defensible, and built upon a solid foundation of archeological and historical evidence. I suppose that is why I become uneasy over certain New Testament descriptions of faith.

> *Now faith is the substance of things hoped for, the evidence of things not seen. (Hebrews 11:1 KJV)*

I don't like that definition. I want faith to be the rational response to evidence that demands a verdict and proof that cannot be refuted. But Scripture offers a very different description. Unimpressed by brains and brawn, it celebrates characteristics I would rather conceal than acknowledge.

> *But God chose the foolish things of the world to shame the wise; God chose the weak things of the world to shame the strong. He chose the lowly things of this world and the despised things—and the things that are not—to nullify the things that are, so that no one may boast before him. (1 Corinthians 1:27–29)*

I don't much like that passage, either. It suggests that those of us following Jesus are foolish, weak, and lowly, not wise, strong, and exalted. I want to be listed among the best and the brightest, to flaunt a high I.Q. and look down my nose at the ignorant folly of unbelief. But God wants something different, a posture that runs completely counter to my natural instinct.

> God opposes the proud but gives grace to the humble.
> (James 4:6)

Faith, no matter how much I want it to be otherwise, has very little to do with what I know or how well I can defend my beliefs. Christianity is not about articulately winning the argument over what is true. It is about humbly submitting the heart to what is real.

⤜

Answers exist for each of the questions and tensions just raised, as well as for other hard sayings of Scripture. But those answers come from believers motivated to resolve the dissonant chords of their faith. I do not question whether we can reconcile biblical hard sayings, but why we want to do so. After all, many unbelievers use these same hard sayings of Scripture to justify opting out rather than trying to resolve tensions that support an unbelieving posture.

Hard to Swallow

The Bible makes some very harsh statements.

CHAPTER 17

The Elephant in the Room

"It is better for you to enter the kingdom of God with one eye than to have two eyes and be thrown into hell."

There is an elephant in the room of Christian theology that cannot be ignored. It is big. It is ugly. And no matter how clear of its potentially crushing step one may stand, it makes us all uneasy. So we might as well face it directly. Jesus did—clearly and forcefully proclaiming its dreadful reality.

> *You snakes! You brood of vipers! How will you escape being condemned to hell? (Matthew 23:33)*

> *The rich man also died and was buried. In hell, where he was in torment, he looked up and saw Abraham far away, with Lazarus by his side. So he called to him, "Father Abraham, have pity on me and send Lazarus to dip the tip of his finger in water and cool my tongue, because I am in agony in this fire." (Luke 16:22–24)*

The apostles also refer to it in their writings, such as Peter's frightening description of what awaits false teachers.

> *In their greed these teachers will exploit you with stories they have made up. Their condemnation has long been hanging*

171

over them, and their destruction has not been sleeping.
For if God did not spare angels when they sinned, but sent
them to hell, putting them into gloomy dungeons to be held
for judgment . . . if he condemned the cities of Sodom and
Gomorrah by burning them to ashes, and made them an
example of what is going to happen to the ungodly . . .
then the Lord knows how to rescue godly men from trials
and to hold the unrighteous for the day of judgment, while
continuing their punishment . . . But these men blaspheme
in matters they do not understand. They are like brute beasts,
creatures of instinct, born only to be caught and destroyed,
and like beasts they too will perish. They will be paid back
with harm for the harm they have done. (2 Peter 2:3–13)

And don't forget John's prophetic summary of how our story
ends.

And I saw the dead, great and small, standing before the
throne, and books were opened . . . The dead were judged
according to what they had done as recorded in the books . . .
Then death and Hades were thrown into the lake of fire. The
lake of fire is the second death. If anyone's name was not
found written in the book of life, he was thrown into the lake
of fire. (Revelation 20:12–15)

Like it or not, Christianity includes the distasteful notion of
eternal damnation. "Hellfire and brimstone" is more than a
Southern Baptist preaching style. To those compelled to believe
the teachings of Jesus and the apostles, it is the unthinkable destiny of millions.

As if the biblical descriptions were not bad enough, a man
named Dante Alighieri came along in the fourteenth century to
craft an imaginative vision of the underworld that has literally
scared the hell out of readers for generations. Its frightening portrait of a dark place specially designed to torment the heathen

and punish the rebel creates a profoundly disturbing aura around the words "eternal damnation."

While touring the circular levels of hell, Dante encounters the anguished screams of the damned. His first journey includes a stroll through upper hell where unbelievers endure punishments specifically suited to their individual crimes. The lustful are blown about in a dark, stormy wind; the gluttonous endure filthy muck while battered with dirty hail, rain, and snow; and the slothful subsist beneath the mud, a bubbling surface the only indication of their endless suffocation below.

Moving further down the underworld tour, the narrator encounters the awful stench of lower hell, where the more serious suffering occurs. Heretics, sodomites, those who committed violence against others and against themselves through suicide, sorcerers, thieves, hypocrites, liars, traitors, and charlatans—all pay for their sins in this place of unrelenting horror and unquenchable fire. Dante's journey through hell's inferno ends when they reach the lowest region where Lucifer, frozen from the chest downward, devours the worst of human sinners. . .

> In each of his three mouths he crunched a sinner,
> with teeth like those that rake the hemp and flax,
> keeping three sinners constantly in pain;
>
> the one in front—the biting he endured
> was nothing like the clawing that he took;
> sometimes his back was raked clean of its skin.
>
> "That soul up there who suffers most of all,"
> my guide explained, "is Judas Iscariot:
> the one with head inside and legs out kicking."[1]

I feel more comfortable accepting the notion of hell when I think of Judas Iscariot or the perpetrators of the Holocaust. My soul cries out for such a place when reading of innocent girls brutally raped and dismembered by a deranged serial killer. I don't want Ted Bundy or Hitler going to heaven. I want them to suffer for the unimaginable pain they have caused.

On the other hand, when I think of loved ones who reject or ignore the gospel until their last breath, I want to interpret hell as mere allegory.

Mark struggles with the idea on both fronts. A committed Christian, he admits to a lifetime of wrestling with the concept of hell—a match he is losing despite an otherwise traditional Protestant theology.

"The punishment doesn't fit the crime!" he almost shouts. His intensity tells me Mark has thought about this for some time. "I mean, even if a person spends seventy or eighty years living the most wicked existence imaginable, an eternity of torment seems extreme."

Mark is a compassionate person, a Christian counselor who ministers to people trapped in the addictive and destructive cycles of sin. He has a hard time condemning those he perceives unable to overcome the pull of evil. While responsible for their actions, he believes, they are still victims to the influence of human fallenness.

"For a person to suffer in flames forever and ever and ever," Mark continues, "how is God glorified in that?"

Many sidestep the harsh nature of biblical descriptions of hell by interpreting them as figurative or hyperbole. Mark would like to join them, but recognizes the problems picking and choosing among Jesus' teachings—accepting those you like while explaining away the rest.

I recall the first time I grasped the concept of hell. I was a small child, probably too young for an R-rated concept like eternal damnation. Sitting in church beside my parents, my greatest fear had been getting caught teasing my brother, chewing the gum I was told to spit out before entering the service, or daydreaming rather than listening to the preacher. That fear quickly paled, however, by a much greater source of anxiety when the minister read what Jesus said about a threatening inferno.

> *If your hand causes you to sin, cut it off. It is better for you to enter life maimed than with two hands to go into hell, where the fire never goes out. And if your foot causes you to sin, cut it off. It is better for you to enter life crippled than to have two feet and be thrown into hell. If your eye causes you to sin, pluck it out. It is better for you to enter the kingdom of God with one eye than to have two eyes and be thrown into hell, where "their worm does not die, and the fire is not quenched." (Mark 9:43–48)*

The prospect of worms that don't die and flames licking at scorchable flesh got my attention. But cutting off my hands and feet or poking out an eye seemed equally scary. Fortunately, the preacher gave me an alternative, suggesting I instead pray the sinner's prayer—a much better option for avoiding such a terrible fate.

More than thirty years later, my fears have shifted from my own eternal destiny to the destiny of others. It feels wonderful to be among millions who have accepted Jesus' gift of salvation, dodging worms and flames in the process. But billions have not, some of whom don't even know they have the option. What about *them*? How can I glibly accept the idea that they face such a dreadful demise?

For starters, I don't accept it glibly. On the contrary, eternal damnation is a sobering reality I hate to acknowledge and would love to deny. I believe it because Jesus taught it, not because I like it. As I said in chapter 16, I wish I didn't believe some things. Hell is among the biggest.

The important question, however, is not whether I believe the hard sayings of the Bible, but why I do so despite disagreeable notions like eternal damnation.

I suppose I accept the hard sayings of Scripture for the same reason I pay eighty dollars for thirty family photos of various sizes, when I really only want the 8x10 and two wallets. You see, they come as a package. To get the two wallets, I need to buy the rest, including more 5x7 photos than I have relatives.

Don't tell her I said so, but my wife has a few irritating habits. When we married, I happily accepted them as part of a wonderful package. Not all do. Some spouses accept only the pleasant parts of their mate and spend years rejecting, criticizing, or resenting the rest. Of course, doing so undermines and eventually destroys a relationship. In the process of spurning bad habits which will never go away, we push away the good. As a result, the sweetness of wedded bliss gets displaced by the biting sting of endless conflict.

Truth comes as a package. I may want only the 8x10 of the Beatitudes and the comfort of certain psalms. But to get them I must buy all of Christianity—redemption as well as damnation, grace along with wrath, "whosoever will" and its counterpart, "no other way."

We mustn't view Christianity like a pair of slippers: hoping it will be warm and cozy when we need a break from the harsh realities of life. C. S. Lewis once discouraged such thinking, acknowledging that parts of the Christian faith make one quite uncomfortable. In his words:

> I wish it was possible to say something more agreeable. But I must say what I think true. Of course, I quite agree that the Christian religion is, in the long run, a thing of unspeakable comfort. But it does not begin in comfort; it begins in the dismay I have been describing, and it is no use at all trying to go on to that comfort without first going through that dismay. In religion, as in war and everything else, comfort is the one thing you cannot get by looking for it. If you look for truth, you may find comfort in the end; if you look for comfort you will not get either

comfort or truth—only soft soap and wishful thinking to begin with and, in the end, despair.[2]

Put simply, Christianity includes some tenets that most Christians dislike, concepts we struggle to accept, let alone defend. But they are part of a wonderful package.

Hard to Swallow

Eternal damnation.

Willful Defiance

—The REBEL—

*Sorry I missed church,
I've been busy practicing witchcraft
and becoming a Lesbian.*

BUMPER STICKER

CHAPTER 18

Insanity

"Better to reign in Hell,
than serve in Heav'n."

A half-crazed, reclusive old man repeatedly screams his victim's name, pleading pardon for his murderous deed. Attendants rush to the room where a once-renowned, long-forgotten musician sits in a pool of his own blood. Adding a botched suicide to his list of failures, the injured gets rushed to the local insane asylum for care and incarceration. A young priest slips beside the recuperating inmate to hear his confession and offer absolution to an obviously lost soul.

So begins the film adaptation of Peter Shaffer's brilliantly crafted play *Amadeus*. Set in eighteenth-century Austria, the story is built around the supposed friendship and rivalry between Wolfgang Amadeus Mozart and his contemporary, Antonio Salieri.

In the play, Salieri is an average talent exalted to the honored position of Court Composer in eighteenth-century Vienna. His one desire in life is to achieve fame by creating, in his words, "Music! Absolute music!" And things seem to be going quite well. The King favors Salieri and his mediocre compositions, making him the most successful young musician in a city of musicians. But then, one day Mozart comes to Vienna—and that changes everything.

Title and status become hollow to Salieri, knowing himself vastly inferior to the young composer from Salzburg. Salieri simply can't create the kind of heaven-inspired music that flows effortlessly from the heart and hand of his competitor. Angry at the God he considers unjust and cruel for giving him the ability to recognize but not create pure music, Salieri voices his contempt.

> I have worked and worked the talent You allowed me . . . Solely that in the end . . . I might hear Your Voice! And now I do hear it—and it says only one name: MOZART! . . . Him you have chosen to be Your sole conduct! And my only reward—my sublime privilege—is to be the sole man alive in this time who shall clearly recognize Your Incarnation! So be it! From this time we are enemies, You and I![1]

And that is precisely what he does. Fueled by the desire to block God's voice, Salieri determines to destroy Mozart by burying his music and, if necessary, his corpse.

> On that dreadful night . . . my life acquired a terrible and thrilling purpose. The blocking of God in one of His purest manifestations. I had the power. God needed Mozart to let Himself into the world. And Mozart needed me to get him worldly advancement. So it would be a battle to the end—and Mozart was the battleground.[2]

But midway through the war, Mozart dies, thus foiling Salieri's strategy. The victory, it seems, is God's. Over the ensuing decades, insanity infests Salieri's once lucid mind. Poisoned by the bitterness that has consumed his life, he concocts one last stroke of diabolical brilliance in order to pry a few scraps of lasting recognition from his divine enemy's clenched fist.

> You see, I cannot accept this. I did not live on earth to be His joke for eternity. I will be remembered! I will be remembered!— if not in fame, then infamy. One moment more and I win my battle with Him. Watch and see! . . . All this month I've been shouting about murder. "Have mercy, Mozart! Pardon your Assassin!"

... And now my last move. A false confession—short and convincing! For the rest of time whenever men say Mozart with love, they will say Salieri with loathing! ... I am going to be immortal after all! And He is powerless to prevent it.[3]

Better to be famously hated than indifferently forgotten.

Shaffer's tragic script creates a sense that one has encountered something deeper, uglier, and more disturbing than a mere tale of petty jealousy. That is because it echoes a much older, greater rivalry.

Paradise Lost

Once upon a time, Lucifer was the highest creation in all of God's domain. None outranked him. No one came near his splendor, strength, cunning, or talent. His role before the rebellion was to lead the created order in its worship of God, as the prophets Ezekiel and Isaiah explain in descriptions traditionally attributed to Lucifer.

> You were the model of perfection, full of wisdom and perfect in beauty ... You were blameless in your ways from the day you were created ... (Ezekiel 28:13–15)

But Lucifer rebelled, choosing to use these gifts to serve and worship himself rather than God.

> You said in your heart, "I will ascend to heaven; I will raise my throne above the stars of God; I will sit enthroned on the mount of assembly, on the utmost heights of the sacred mountain. I will ascend above the tops of the clouds; I will make myself like the Most High." (Isaiah 14:13–14)

This is the insanity of pride, the reason for our last category of unbeliever: the rebel. One spoken into existence by God saw himself as God's equal. Unwilling to remain an honored servant, Lucifer made a play for the top role. What he considered a noble war against an arrogant tyrant was in truth a delusional boycott of reality, mad as a mouse declaring himself to be a lion, foolish as a tree cutting itself off from its life-sustaining roots.

So Lucifer gave birth to a death that is not the end of existence, but the beginning of something far worse: an eternity of madness, separated from the source of sanity.

> *Your heart became proud on account of your beauty, and you corrupted your wisdom because of your splendor. (Ezek 28:17)*

Notice the consequence of Lucifer's mutiny: "You corrupted your wisdom." Insanity, by definition, is losing touch with reality. Lucifer began going mad the moment he rejected the ultimate reality of God's supreme rule.

And so Lucifer lost his exalted post. Banished. Thrown out. Defeated. Punished. Dishonored. Call it what you will. The once dignified servant named Lucifer became a disgraced outcast known as Satan, Beelzebub, Serpent, and the Devil.

> *I drove you in disgrace from the mount of God, and I expelled you, O guardian cherub, from among the fiery stones.*
> *(Ezekiel 28:16)*
>
> *I threw you to the earth; I made a spectacle of you . . .*
> *(Ezekiel 28:17)*
>
> *You were brought down to the grave, to the depths of the pit.*
> *(Isaiah 14:16)*

But Lucifer never accepted his defeat, nor submitted to the reality that was, is, and will always be: "The Lord is One."

Adding insult to injury, God made man in his own image, unseating Lucifer as the highest object of angelic admiration and wonder. Like Mozart arriving in Vienna, a new musician entered the scene. Satan hates us because we bear the image of his enemy, making us a continual reminder of his mediocrity. And by taking the attention off of him, we became the focus of his rage.

His strategy for getting back on top? Mar the innocent beauty we possess. Make us into something we were never made to be. Invite us to join him in the insanity of rebellion.

In the year 1663, English poet John Milton completed his five-year effort to write what is widely considered one of the all time great literary achievements. His epic poem *Paradise Lost* was intended, in Milton's words, to "assert Eternal Providence, And justify the ways of God to men." The central themes of this masterpiece are the rebellion of Lucifer and his effort to undermine God's plan for mankind.

In what has become one of the most famous passages of this epic work, Milton paints a picture of what it must have been like among the fallen angelic beings that had joined Lucifer's failed coup attempt, only to find themselves cast into hell along with their leader. In an effort to comfort them with the hope of yet regaining supremacy, Lucifer raises his fist to God's throne and declares. . .

> *Here we may reign secure, and in my choice*
> *To reign is worth ambition though in Hell:*
> *Better to reign in Hell, than serve in Heav'n.*[4]

Lucifer dedicated his entire existence to thwarting God's purposes and plans, preferring first chair in hell to heaven's second fiddle. So he commissioned his fallen host to the task of undermining God-designed goodness with the evil that is its absence.

> *Fall'n Cherub, to be weak is miserable*
> *Doing or Suffering: but of this be sure,*
> *To do aught good never will be our task,*
> *But ever to do ill our sole delight,*
> *As being the contrary to his high will*
> *Whom we resist. If then his Providence*
> *Out of our evil seek to bring forth good,*
> *Our labour must be to pervert that end,*
> *And out of good still to find means of evil.*[5]

I have often wondered what could possibly keep Satan motivated in light of his obvious inability to defeat the supreme power of Almighty God. Milton finds the answer in Lucifer's belief that he will "out of good still to find means of evil."

One such evil involves enlisting men and women in his rebellion against reality. The means of recruiting? You guessed it: lies. Like the one in the garden of Eden.

> You will not surely die," the serpent said to the woman. "For God knows that when you eat of it your eyes will be opened, and you will be like God . . ." (Genesis 3:4–5)

In his excellent book *Behind the Glittering Mask*, Mark Rutland depicts a debate between Lucifer and Michael the archangel. One portion of the argument reveals a Lucifer so dedicated to his own propaganda that he can no longer acknowledge a reality he once proclaimed.

MICHAEL: You accuse God of Pride?

LUCIFER: Of course. Monstrous Pride. Has there ever been such a self-absorbed, demanding ego? Everything must praise him. Those of us who would not constantly bathe his ego in worship were exiled. Only those of you who would bow and scrape could stay. Don't you ever chafe? Don't you ever think all that "You're Perfect" "You're Holy" "You're Lovely" is just a bit cloying? . . . What about his pride?[6]

Michael reminds Lucifer that it is not proud for a rabbit to think himself a rabbit, or an angel to believe himself an angel. But for a mouse to think himself a lion is delusional pride. Ultimate reality, he points out, is that God is God.

MICHAEL: I only know that the Lord, He is God. It is He who made us. We did not make ourselves. And we most certainly did not make Him. He is God. Not to worship Him is insane pride.

LUCIFER: Why must there be only one god?

MICHAEL: Why indeed? Must is not the question. That is simply the way it is. There are billions of rabbits who know themselves to be rabbits. There are billions of mice and mules and men. And there are legions of angels. As long as they know themselves to be mice or men or angels, all is well. But when they think themselves to be gods, the madness of your rebellion eats out their insides.[7]

When we rebel against God, we mimic an unbelief that begins and ends with madness. Like Salieri demanding infamy through a lie, Lucifer chose the path of deception for himself and his followers. "When he lies, he speaks his native language," Jesus explained. "He is a liar. And the father of lies." He lies to himself. He lied in Eden. His lies will continue until the day he faces that inevitable, deadly thud guaranteed by rebellion's leap off the cliff of sanity. And sadly, his will not be the only soul broken on its ragged, rocky bottom.

Hard To Swallow

There is only one God.

CHAPTER 19

Highway to Hell

"The idea of heaven is just Christianity's way
of creating hell on earth."

I endured adolescence during the seventies, a compliant Baptist with short hair in the heyday of long-haired rebellion. A band called KISS was at the height of popularity. According to unsubstantiated legend, the name stood for "Kids In Satan's Service"—which seemed likely to us since the group was famous for demonic makeup, wild music, and drug-infested sex parties. I even got beat up by one of their fans, a guy who wore KISS T-shirts to school on days the rest of his wardrobe (Alice Cooper and AC/DC attire) decomposed at the bottom of the laundry pile.

During my sophomore year, AC/DC released its *Highway to Hell* album, confirming my suspicion that heavy metal artists served Satan himself. I figured you must be up to no good if your fans pummel the religiously devout.

Not every kid wearing heavy metal attire was bad. Most of them just wanted to appear cool, mindlessly following the crowd to the latest band feeding predictable adolescent appetites for edgy, over-the-top, shock-my-parents rebellion. But some had a deeper motivation, announcing to the world that they had deserted the God of Vacation Bible School days and joined the enemy camp—an attitude reflected in their language, their demeanor, their grades, and on their T-shirts.

I remember wondering why anyone would align himself with one the Bible describes as a roaring lion seeking someone to devour. From all appearances, they knew exactly what they were doing, defiantly sticking their heads into the lion's gaping mouth to show themselves fearless. A good number of them (kids we called "burnouts") zealously followed the self-destructive path their rock heroes extolled, celebrating themes clearly intended to offend common decency and mock Christian ideals.

I recall wondering whether those kids were passively misguided or willfully defiant, blind sheep stumbling off a cliff or eager wolves leaping for the thrill of the fall. Do people consciously choose to reject God, knowing the dire consequences, or have they inadvertently stepped in spiritual quicksand?

Brian Warner had a KISS poster on his bedroom wall during the 1970s, something the Heritage Christian School faculty would have frowned upon if discovered. But Brian didn't care; his resentment for religious rules and instruction prompted many a prank, including the time he placed his grandfather's sex toys in his teacher's top drawer, hoping for expulsion to the freedom of public school. Eventually he succeeded and Brian escaped green pastures to pursue browner grass on the other side of the fence. In his words:

> Christian school had prepared me well for public school. It defined the taboos, then held them away at arm's length, leaving me reaching for them in vain. As soon as I switched schools, it was all there for the taking—sex, drugs, rock, the occult. I didn't even have to look for them: They found me.[1]

Brian went on to become one of the most outrageous rock stars of the '90s. Better known by his assumed name, Marilyn Manson, his image and antics make his shock ancestors look quaint by comparison. Manson's carefully crafted persona celebrates transvestite sexuality and obsessive morbidity. He appears part decaying corpse, part licentious demon—like something out of your worst nightmare. It is chillingly fitting that one of his hottest albums bears the name *Antichrist Superstar*.

In an unpleasant bit of research, I read Manson's photo-laced autobiography titled *The Long Hard Road Out of Hell.* The book repeatedly references Dante's *Inferno,* suggesting a life journey spiraling downward alongside the worst of the damned, complete with a series of personal anecdotes describing sexual debauchery, illicit drug use, and offensive reflections so foul one can almost smell the stench of a life consumed by pathetically hollow pursuits.

But Manson's book also invites readers inside the head of one drawn to the darkest of the dark, a pattern that started when an adolescent kid rebelled against Christian teachers' attempts to protect young Brian from the dangerous world of sex, drugs, and rock and roll.

> They would bring in Led Zeppelin, Black Sabbath, and Alice Cooper records and play them loudly on the P.A. system. Different teachers would take turns at the record player, spinning the albums backward with an index finger and explaining the hidden messages. Of course, the most extreme music with the most satanic messages was exactly what I wanted to listen to, chiefly because it was forbidden. They would hold up photographs of the bands to frighten us, but all that ever accomplished was to make me decide that I wanted long hair and an earring just like the rockers in the pictures.[2]

It didn't take long for Brian's spiral to accelerate beyond passive admiration into a consuming pursuit of all things illicit and occult. While reading Milton's *Paradise Lost* during high school, Brian found himself admiring Lucifer more than God. Not that he necessarily believes in a literal Satan. In Manson's words:

> The devil doesn't exist. Satanism is about worshipping yourself, because you are responsible for your own good and evil. Christianity's war against the devil has always been a fight

against man's most natural instincts—for sex, for violence, for self-gratification—and a denial of man's membership in the animal kingdom. The idea of heaven is just Christianity's way of creating a hell on earth.[3]

Perhaps that is why he explained launching his shocking rock image "because there didn't seem like any other way to snap society out of its Christianity induced coma."[4]

Clearly, Manson is no victim. He is a rebel.

Conscious Rejection

One need only read as far as the third chapter of the Bible to realize men and women can consciously reject good, choosing the thrill of the fall over the security of the bridge.

Imagine everything you could ever want being placed before you with the invitation to enjoy it all. You may partake as much, as often, and as long as you like. No limits. No guilt. No calories. The only concession on your part is to stay away from one tree with a particular type of fruit. Anything and everything in the world in exchange for one restriction. Adam and Eve were given that choice.

The forbidden fruit symbolized mankind's freedom to accept or reject God's offer of intimacy. God placed the tree in the garden not to tempt but to testify, a daily reminder to Adam and Eve that they could enjoy God's loving protection or chart their own course. The choice was made clear and the consequences explained.

> And the LORD God commanded the man, "You are free to eat from any tree in the garden; but you must not eat from the tree of the knowledge of good and evil, for when you eat of it you will surely die." (Genesis 2:16–17)

So what did Adam do? He took a big bite of the fruit. A mistake? Hardly. He made a deliberate choice to spurn God's offer of protective love, a decision that would determine the course of all human history by planting a seed within each of us that grows into an ugly, strangling weed called rebellion.

I consider myself an optimist who tries to give people the benefit of the doubt. I like to think that most people would submit to the truth if they only understood it. Ignorance or confusion drive poor choices, not premeditated rebellion. If only they were given indisputable evidence and dummy-proof instructions, they would accept God's gracious gift. That is what I would like to think.

Unfortunately, that is not the reality.

Pharaoh saw the miracle of the plagues, yet hardened his heart against the God of Israel.

The children of Israel saw the miracles leading to their freedom from bondage, and then their provision in the wilderness, yet crafted a golden calf to worship instead of their clearly superior God.

Or consider perhaps the most striking case in point: the religious leaders of Jesus' day. Immediately after witnessing some of his most dramatic miracles, they did the last thing you might expect.

> Then he said to the man, "Stretch out your hand." So he stretched it out and it was completely restored, just as sound as the other. But the Pharisees went out and plotted how they might kill Jesus. (Matthew 12:13–14)

Rather than fall down on their faces to worship Jesus in awe and reverence for his demonstration of divine power, they plotted his death. When confronted by God's reality face-to-face, some try to destroy the evidence—something they did in another, even more shocking example as described in the twelfth chapter of John's gospel.

After Jesus raised Lazarus from the dead, the chief priests made plans to put him back in the grave because word of the miracle caused many to follow Jesus. Hard as it is to accept, when God makes himself known in dramatic fashion, some resist him all the more.

> *Even after Jesus had done all these miraculous signs in their presence, they still would not believe in him. (John 12:37)*

I would like to give people the benefit of the doubt. But some make it very hard to do so.

A Devilish Deal

Why settle for the mundane when you can easily have excitement? Why work long hours for a paycheck when you can acquire great wealth at the drop of a hat? Why grapple for recognition or influence when fame and power can be handed to you on a silver platter? Why restrict yourself to fidelity when just by asking you can enjoy the uninhibited indulgence of variety? Why accept boring old reality when fantasy offers far more fun?

Such questions have characterized the lure of high living since the beginning of time, and a deal offered by the devil himself in numerous stories, one of the most famous penned by English playwright and Shakespeare contemporary Christopher Marlowe. *The Tragical History of Doctor Faustus* tells of a man dissatisfied with his lot in life, consumed by lust for power, wealth, and fame. In the words of the play's central protagonist:

> *Ay, these are those that Faustus most desires.*
> *O, what a world of profit and delight,*
> *Of power, of honour, of omnipotence,*
> *Is promised to the studious artizan!*[5]

Bored by the tedious yet legitimate disciplines of law, philosophy, theology, and other studies reflecting divine restrictions on human pursuits, Faustus willingly takes a forbidden shortcut to his goals by mastering the dark arts.

A sound magician is a mighty god:
Here, Faustus, tire thy brains to gain a deity!
. . . Philosophy is odious and obscure;
Both law and physic are for petty wits;
Divinity is basest of the three,
Unpleasant, harsh, contemptible, and vile:
'Tis magic, magic, that hath ravish'd me.[6]

As Faustus pores over his books, a good angel and a demon join the Doctor in his study. The former warns that such blasphemous pursuits invite God's wrath. The latter encourages going forward in the dark arts and learning to control nature's mysterious elements.

Heeding the advice that best quenches his wicked thirst, Faustus conjures up one of hell's servants with a chillingly profane incantation.

Away with the triple deity of Jehovah! Hail, spirits of fire,
air, water and earth! Prince of the East (Lucifer),
Belzebub, monarch of burning hell, and Demigorgon,
we propitiate you, that Mephistophilis may appear and rise.

Mephistophilis emerges at Faustus' request in the garb of a Franciscan Friar. Faustus' petition is simple. He asks Mephistophilis to wait upon his every command as would a genie freed from the bottle. Hell's servant must seek permission from the Prince of Darkness before granting such a request.

FAUSTUS: Now tell me what says Lucifer, thy lord?
MEPH: That I shall wait on Faustus while he lives,
So he will buy my service with his soul . . .
Thou must bequeath it solemnly,
And write a deed of gift with thine own blood.[7]

So goes the devilish deal. You can have a lifetime of wealth, fame, power, and orgies. But there is one stipulation. They come in exchange for your eternal soul.

MEPH: But tell me, Faustus, shall I have thy soul?
And I will be thy slave, and wait on thee,
And give thee more than thou hast wit to ask.
FAUSTUS: Ay, Mephistophilis, I give it thee.[8]

And so, the Doctor takes a shortcut to his dreams. But, in the words of Aslan of Narnia, "All get what they want. They do not always like it."

Few literary scenes are as pitiful as the aged Doctor Faustus' mourning the pending torment of his everlasting soul as he takes his final earthly breath. Nor as instructive as the epilogue with Marlowe's grave admonition...

Faustus is gone: regard his hellish fall,
Whose fiendful fortune may exhort the wise,
Only to wonder at unlawful things,
Whose deepness doth entice such forward wits
To practise more than heavenly power permits.[9]

Countless tales echo the theme of Marlowe's famous play, including *The Devil and Daniel Webster* by Stephen Vincent Benet, in which a poor farmer is offered a similar contract. Down on his luck, the farmer sells his immortal soul to the devil for seven years of fortune, concluding with a courtroom battle between the infamous Daniel Webster and the Devil himself. The story was put to film in 1941 and again in the 1981 comedic retelling titled *The Devil and Max Devlin*, starring Bill Cosby.

In *The Devil's Advocate*, by Andrew Neiderman, a promising young lawyer is lured by criminal defense attorney John Milton to gain wealth and status by successfully representing the vilest of the vile. As it turns out, John Milton is actually the Devil trying to seduce his young protégé into choosing the temporary pleasures of sin over the boring bliss of blessedness.

Yet another variation shows up in Oscar Wilde's *The Picture of Dorian Gray*—the tale of a handsome young playboy who enjoys a reckless, self-destructive lifestyle of pleasure while bearing none of the physical marks of aging and corruption his soul accumulates over time. His face and body remain ever perfect, the deterioration transferred instead to a portrait hidden safely away in his attic. The young man eventually goes mad, killing himself in a fit of well-earned remorse.

Different twists on the same idea: our tendency to choose immediate gratification over long-term joy, and that deep-seated human drive to transcend what ought to be. More than mere literary devices, these themes reflect real choices made by real people who willfully reject God's gracious gifts.

Day Trip from Hell

In one of my all-time favorite books, *The Great Divorce*, C. S. Lewis tells the story of what happens to a group of hell's inhabitants loaded onto a bus for a day visit to heaven. Most go reluctantly, used to the misery they inhabit. A misery, after all, they have carefully fashioned for some time.

Upon arrival, the visitors complain about the sharp edge of reality that cuts the tender soles of their feet, and how the brightness of true light offends their eyes. Most find the true beauty of heaven's perimeter a disagreeable sight, and wonder why anyone would choose to inhabit such a harsh domain.

As in Dante's epic poem that inspired *The Great Divorce*, Lewis is guided through the afterworld by a great poet who explains the dilemma of the damned. One by one, Lewis and his guide eavesdrop on conversations between the ghostly visitors and those heavenly residents he calls Solid People. You quickly learn of the countless techniques, excuses, and self-deceptions of those desperate to avoid ultimate realities, such as universal truth and selfless love.

Lewis' guide explains that the despicable, miserable creatures he observes were not condemned to hell by God's tyrannical rule, but by their own choice.

There are only two kinds of people in the end: those who say to God, "Thy will be done," and those to whom God says, in the end, "Thy will be done." All that are in Hell, choose it.[10]

Again, when we reject the good that God is, we embrace the evil he isn't. As Lewis' guide further explains:

There is but one good; that is God. Everything else is good when it looks to Him and bad when it turns from Him. And the higher and mightier it is in the natural order, the more demoniac it will be if it rebels. It's not out of bad mice or bad fleas you make demons, but out of bad archangels.[11]

The chilling reality is this: since man ranks above archangels in God's hierarchy of creation, we too can become demons . . . or something worse.

Glorious Indulgence

"On Saturday night I would see men lusting after half-naked girls dancing at the carnival," a young Anton recalls from his days as a circus musician, "and on Sunday morning when I was playing the organ for tent-show evangelists at the other end of the carnival lot, I would see these same men sitting in the pews with their wives and children, asking God to forgive them and purge them of carnal desires. And the next Saturday night they'd be back at the carnival or some other place of indulgence."

Such experiences drove that young man to two conclusions. First, Christianity thrives on hypocrisy; second, man's carnal nature will always dominate his existence. Both would become foundational to his philosophy of life, a life exemplifying just how far our propensity toward rebellion can bring us.

In April of 1966, thirty-six-year-old Anton Szandor LaVey announced the formation of the Church of Satan. A few years later he published *The Satanic Bible*, in which he recorded what would become the governing orthodoxy of a new sect with very

198 ✿ The REBEL

old roots. He intended to elevate the dark arts from their historical place, lurking in the cultural shadows, to one of mainstream legitimacy—a legacy his church continues years after his 1997 death, as reflected on its internet homepage.

> Welcome to the official website of the Church of Satan. Founded on April 30, 1966 c.e. by Anton Szandor LaVey, we are the first above-ground organization in history openly dedicated to the acceptance of Man's true nature—that of a carnal beast, living in a cosmos which is permeated and motivated by the Dark Force which we call Satan. Over the course of time, Man has called this Force by many names, and it has been reviled by those whose very nature causes them to be separate from this fountainhead of existence. They live in obsessive envy of we who exist by flowing naturally with the dread Prince of Darkness. It is for this reason that individuals who resonate with Satan have always been an alien elite, often outsiders in cultures whose masses pursue solace in an external deity. We Satanists are our own Gods, and we are the explorers of the Left-Hand Path. We do not bow down before the myths and fictions of the desiccated spiritual followers of the Right-Hand Path.

Beyond initiating a left-handed elite, LaVey sought to free his flock from religiously motivated prohibitions against carnal delights. He encouraged the worship of fleshly things because they "produce pleasure" and create a temple of "glorious indulgence." In fact, two of his nine "Satanic Statements"—loosely imitating a creed—oppose the Christian notions of self-sacrifice and self-restraint.

- Statement One: Satan represents indulgence, instead of abstinence!
- Statement Eight: Satan represents all of the so-called sins, as they all lead to physical, mental, or emotional gratification!

Though he described Satan as "the spirit of revolt that leads to freedom" and "the embodiment of all heresies that liberate," LaVey denied the existence of a literal, personal Lucifer. He called that doctrine of Satan the best friend the church ever had by keeping it in business. His chosen path involved "revolt" leading to "freedom," driven by a deep contempt for the God of Christianity, as a few distasteful morsels from his *Book of Satan* reveal.

- Chapter I, Verse 6: "I dip my forefinger in the watery blood of your impotent mad redeemer, and write over his thorn-torn brow: The TRUE prince of evil—the king of the slaves!"
- I, Verse 10: "I gaze into the glassy eye of your fearsome Jehovah, and pluck him by the beard; I uplift a broad-axe, and split open his worm-eaten skull!"
- II, Verse 1: "Behold the crucifix; what does it symbolize? Pallid incompetence hanging on a tree."

As High Priest of the Church of Satan, nicknamed "The Black Pope" by many, Anton LaVey led his followers in conscious, willful rebellion against everything sacred to Christians. Like Doctor Faustus, his passion to control the power of the dark arts and to break free of God's protective restrictions drove choices only the naïve could label mistakes. His own writings don't give that option.

Anton LaVey had many kindred spirits, including a young Marilyn Manson, who called LaVey a father figure. The shock rocker shared a similar life mission with the Church of Satan founder, admitting both had dedicated the better part of their lives to toppling Christianity.[12]

Clearly, both men knew what they were doing and invited others to join them. They are the extreme representatives of millions who, for one reason or another, deliberately steer their lives onto the highway to hell.

I'm on the highway to Hell
No stop signs, speed limit
Nobody's gonna slow me down...
I'm going down, all the way down
I'm on the highway to Hell.

Hard To Swallow

God calls fun evil.

Why Unbelief?
—CONCLUSIONS—

*We are often unable to tell people what
they need to know because they want
to know something else and would therefore
only misunderstand what we said.*

GEORGE MACDONALD

CHAPTER 20

Recovering Unbeliever

Throughout this book we have encountered a variety of reasons people consider Christianity hard to swallow. Disillusionment drove Mary Ellen away from the faith she once loved. Tactless believers offended Wil, leaving a bad taste in his mouth. We heard from self-described seekers who don't want to find, hard-nosed skeptics who parrot the party line, and famous antagonists who belittle a religion they despise. Some hate Christianity enough to shout profane ramblings, while others convey apathy with an indifferent yawn.

The year I've spent interviewing, studying, and contemplating unbelief has both challenged and affirmed my own faith. I must admit, however, that diving deep into the waters of doubt and skepticism has left me in need of air. I desperately want to resurface and refresh my oxygen-starved spirit.

But the process has done me good. I've checked the locks and found no surprises, allowing me to settle back into confident faith. But I do so more aware and perplexed than ever of how difficult it is for some to believe.

Mary Ellen and Jonathan point to unmet expectations, but millions believe despite far more intense disappointment.

Wil and Olive took offense at rude or wayward Christians, so each walked away from the church. And while I understand their feelings, I don't understand their decision. I've been offended and disappointed by the behavior of believers over and over again. But I still believe. Cloudy days don't make me renounce the sun.

For every person who rejects Christianity, you can find someone else with the same experience or objection who believes.

A skeptic named Nietzsche gleefully declared God dead. A former skeptic named C. S. Lewis reluctantly declared himself wrong.

A bullying heckler named Voltaire considered reason a weapon against faith. A believing philosopher named Pascal said, "the heart has reasons which are unknown to reason."

A bright nineteenth-century writer named Mark Twain bitterly attacked God as uncaring and unjust in response to painful loss. His equally brilliant contemporary, Leo Tolstoy, responded to bitter disappointment by turning to Christ.

Clearly, more lies behind unbelief than the reasons given. Perhaps more than can be understood.

Have you ever encountered a "lazy eye" picture—the ones with arbitrary dots obscuring a veiled image? They say the key to seeing the true picture is relaxing your eyes. The harder you try, the less likely the hidden figure will reveal itself. Well, I have tried and tried, but have never seen the alleged image. Not once. And nothing feels more frustrating than when everyone else discovers the buried treasure and reacts in gleeful surprise, while my futile gaze makes me cross-eyed.

I wonder whether something similar happens with unbelievers. Do they peer into the microscope or stare at the heavens, hoping to see the purported glory of God, only to go cross-eyed in frustration? Why does the same reality that prompts me to worship the Creator cause them to question his existence? Why is it that, as the apostle John writes, "The light shines in the darkness, but the darkness has not understood it"?

I posed that question to a number of long-term Christians, asking what they consider the most common reasons for unbelief. Many cited misunderstanding, ignorance, or confusion about the content and meaning of the gospel. Certainly, many still need to hear the good news. But that does not explain why others reject it. Some, like Ken in chapter seven, could explain Christianity to me better than many long-term believers. They clearly get it. They just don't buy it.

The most commonly listed culprit, surprisingly, was the church itself. Despite a diverse representation of many denominations, most pinned the blame for others rejecting Christ on us Christians. We simply represent him poorly. The trouble with this scapegoat, as I see it, is that it fails to consider a glaringly obvious reality: millions of people, myself included, have embraced Christianity through the church despite its warts and failures. Looking past offensive remarks, fallen leaders, hypocritical members, and periodic scandals, we still embrace the truth. If poor representation caused unbelief, there would be no believers at all. The church would have died in the first century due to Peter's hot temper or Paul's bad breath.

I wrote this book in order to learn—not teach. It would be arrogant to think myself capable of understanding, let alone answering, every objection to the faith or pinpointing the root cause of unbelief. But I have been forced to confront a dissonant chord that, until now, I have left hanging in the air.

The Election Suggestion

Most believers I questioned raised a potential cause I would love to avoid but feel obliged to address.

"Isn't predestination behind unbelief?"

"Aren't some chosen for God and others for damnation?"

Unsettling questions, but difficult to dismiss in light of certain scriptural passages, such as the one where Jesus reacted to the stubborn unbelief of the religious leaders of his own day:

> No one can come to me unless the Father who sent me draws him. (John 6:44)

And later when he said to a group of believers . . . .

You did not choose me, but I chose you to go and bear fruit—
fruit that will last. (John 15:16)

At first glance, it appears that the game is rigged—a perception even more difficult to avoid when reading from the apostle Paul's writings.

For those God foreknew he also predestined to be conformed
to the likeness of his Son, that he might be the firstborn
among many brothers. And those he predestined, he also
called; those he called, he also justified; those he justified, he
also glorified. (Romans 8:29–30)

In him we were also chosen, having been predestined
according to the plan of him who works out everything in
conformity with the purpose of his will. (Ephesians 1:11)

And then there is the brief but troubling verse found in the book of Acts.

When the Gentiles heard this, they were glad and honored the
word of the Lord: and all who were appointed for eternal life
believed. (Acts 13:48)

Such statements make it easy to assume the whole thing a farce, with God pulling all the strings and making all the decisions. But that notion doesn't ring true when I consider that Jesus went to the cross in order to make salvation possible.

Unbelief must be a free choice, not an inevitable condition. I found it helpful to re-read every biblical passage that uses the terms "elect" and "predestined" in order to wrestle with this question. Most often the terms are used in the context of a specific individual or group selected for a specific purpose, such as the twelve disciples whom God called to a unique role.

It became clear that God does intervene in human affairs and selects whom he wills to accomplish his redemptive purposes. He selected Noah to preserve the human race. He called Abraham to father a people he would use to bless all nations. He used Moses rather than Aaron to lead Israel out of bondage. He selected Peter from among many fishermen and Matthew from among many tax collectors to pen his Scriptures and lead his followers. The word "elect" is even applied to certain angels in 1 Timothy 5:21. Angels do not need salvation, but they do serve God's purposes. Each "election" amounted to God "choosing" from among many to fulfill "the plan of him who works out everything in conformity with the purpose of his will."

Sometimes, "in conformity with the purpose of his will" includes divine choices that sober my spirit. Do you recall the story of Pharaoh when confronted with Moses' command to "let my people go"? Despite clear evidence that the God of Israel was who he claimed to be and that he was serious about the command, Pharaoh refused. After each of the first five plagues, the Scriptures tell us that "Pharaoh hardened his heart and would not let the people go." But then a subtle, yet profound change occurs. Following the sixth plague, we hear that "the Lord hardened Pharaoh's heart . . ."

In the beginning, Egypt's ruler had a choice. He could have cooperated with God in freeing the Hebrews. But when he didn't, God took over and used Pharaoh's resistance for his own awesome and dreadful purposes.

We may choose to remove the dam's first brick, but we won't be able to stop the ensuing flood. Every person makes daily choices that move him or her further down the addictive pattern of unbelief or the liberating discipline of belief. One can resist his natural propensity by submitting to truth, or succumb to that propensity and so disfigure his very soul.

Pharaoh's destiny conformed to that which he willingly chose—a sobering thought when you consider Paul's letter to the Romans in which he tells us that the Lord is patient with everyone . . . up to a point. But when a person shows no intention of repentance, God will "give them over" to the consequence of their chosen path, be it sexual addiction, a depraved mind, or as in Pharaoh's case, national devastation.

This perspective helped me read some of the more challenging biblical passages with new eyes—including a statement in John's gospel that suggests what many consider the unthinkable.

> *Even after Jesus had done all these miraculous signs in their presence, they still would not believe in him ... For this reason they could not believe, because, as Isaiah says elsewhere: "He has blinded their eyes and deadened their hearts, so they can neither see with their eyes, nor understand with their hearts, nor turn—and I would heal them." (John 12:37–40)*

A troubling admission—God does blind the eyes of some to prevent their belief! But then I recall the situation with Pharaoh. He had already hardened his own heart and crossed a line that made him available for God's negative use in a larger story of redemption. Similarly, the Jewish religious leaders had hardened their hearts to Messiah. Apparently, like Pharaoh, they crossed a line that made them available for a dastardly part in the larger redemption story—putting Jesus on the cross. Having already chosen to reject Jesus, God chose them to orchestrate part of his plan.

An alcoholic may choose the bottle as a means of temporary comfort or escape. But at some point, he crosses the line of addiction and the choice is no longer his. The Scriptures clearly tell us that everyone receives ample revelation and opportunity to choose belief or rebellion (Romans 1). But like any other addiction, we can cross a line when the natural pattern of that choice overpowers our will, warps our desires, and forces a patient God to finally say, "thy will be done."

God is a lover, not a rapist. He won't force himself on anyone.

I don't want to bog down in the fine points of theology or enter the eternal debate over the supposed Calvinist and

Armenian positions on such matters. But I did discover that diverse views exist on the meaning of election and predestination, all considered legitimate within the realm of orthodoxy. None of them, however, champion the idea that unbelief is the result of God fixing the game. All acknowledge that the overwhelming emphasis of Scripture includes God's genuine invitation and man's authentic choice. Being chosen for an assignment is very different from being chosen for damnation.

> *This is good, and pleases God our Savior, who wants all men to be saved and to come to a knowledge of the truth. (1 Timothy 2:3–4)*

I do not perceive us to be passive participants in a predetermined outcome. I don't think people reject Christianity because God barricades the door of belief. Nor do they reject it due to disillusionment, offense, skepticism, apathy, or any of the objections cited throughout this book. Certainly, such factors play a role in the drama of individual choice, but they do not unearth the root, in my view. Otherwise none would believe, since all encounter similar disappointments, offenses, perceptions, and hang-ups.

Uncovering the Root

What, then, might we find at the root? When Adam, our forefather and representative, tasted the fruit, he took the first sip of a drink that would come to intoxicate the entire race: rebellion. At that moment, a propensity toward unbelief and disobedience entered our gene pool.

If you give an alcoholic a shot of whisky, you feed his self-destruction. If you offer someone a reason to reject truth, you feed his compulsion to self-deceive. Those of us with alcoholic loved ones understand this all too well. Some better hide their addiction than others; perhaps they get weepy and solitary when drunk. Others get vocal and violent, making it clear to the whole world that they have a problem. No matter how it gets expressed, however, the root remains the same. The bottle is in control.

Some quietly conceal their rebellion, perhaps silently suffering with heartache, like the pain of lost love. But no matter how it expresses itself, unbelief is in control.

For any addiction, the sooner one succumbs, the harder it is to break free. I believe that is part of the reason the vast majority of those who profess Christian faith do so as children. They learn early to avoid the addictive cycle. Talk to anyone trying to quit smoking on their fortieth day without a cigarette, and you will find them much less stressed than on day four. The more time one spends away from the controlling influence, the easier it is to remain free. That is why, in my view, it is much more difficult for an entrenched adult to repent than a child. The former remains firmly in the grasp of his addiction, requiring great effort to break free. The latter has yet to nurture the propensity.

I cannot reach any other conclusion about unbelief than this. Our common tendency toward rebellion and associated addictive patterns drives many to seek justification for an unbelieving posture they desperately want to maintain, clinging to pretext like a drunk to his last swig.

I do not think that every unbeliever knowingly rejects obvious truth. Most of those I interviewed did not willfully shut their eyes to an oncoming train. But their eyes remain closed nonetheless. I do not think they lied to me. But I fear they have been lying to themselves.

The human psyche is highly complex, with the capacity for wonderful heights and frightening depths, great self-awareness and self-delusion, conscious choice and subconscious bondage. We simply cannot untangle the countless influences, compulsions, abilities, and limitations that contribute to one person choosing belief and another unbelief. We can, however, try to understand the factors common to us all. Such as recognizing we are all created in the image of God and carry within our being the lingering echo of his personhood, including senses that perceive and minds that reason.

> *For since the creation of the world God's invisible qualities— his eternal power and divine nature—have been clearly seen, being understood from what has been made, so that men are without excuse. (Romans 1:20)*

We know ourselves to be fallen beings, a marred beauty made less than intended due to rebellion against what ought to be— even to the point of choosing the insanity of lies.

> *For although they knew God, they neither glorified him as God nor gave thanks to him, but their thinking became futile and their foolish hearts were darkened. Although they claimed to be wise, they became fools ... They exchanged the truth of God for a lie, and worshiped and served created things rather than the Creator—who is forever praised. (Romans 1:21–25)*

This pattern mirrors our struggle with other addictive patterns that the apostle Paul attributed to our fallen nature.

> *For I have the desire to do what is good, but I cannot carry it out. For what I do is not the good I want to do; no, the evil I do not want to do—this I keep on doing ... So I find this law at work: When I want to do good, evil is right there with me. For in my inner being I delight in God's law; but I see another law at work in the members of my body, waging war against the law of my mind and making me a prisoner of the law of sin at work within my members. What a wretched man I am! Who will rescue me from this body of death? (Romans 7:18–24)*

Finally, we know that failing to resist our natural propensity makes sin our slave master.

The mind of sinful man is death, but the mind controlled by
the Spirit is life and peace; the sinful mind is hostile to God.
It does not submit to God's law, nor can it do so. Those
controlled by the sinful nature cannot please God. (Romans
8:6–8)

When it comes to deciding to accept or reject Christianity, we are not dispassionate consumers evaluating options, as if choosing a brand of cereal from the store shelf. We are addicts deciding whether to pop another pill or to enter rehab. And the sooner we choose the rehab of belief, the shorter our trip back to clear-headed sanity.

Here's the hard reality: I am a recovering unbeliever. And like any other addict, acknowledging my problem is the first step toward overcoming its stranglehold on my spirit.

Lessons from the Unconvinced

When all is said and done, what does it matter? How does exploring the reasons and root of unbelief affect my own faith walk or how I relate to others? I take several lessons from my time among the unconvinced.

Stop Accepting Blame: It is time I stop blaming myself and the rest of the church for unbelief. We may not be the nicest people all the time, or have the most convincing argument when needed, or wrap the gospel in the prettiest package. We may have embarrassing episodes in our history and inept representatives in some of our pulpits. But we do not *cause* anyone to reject Christianity, any more than the local pub *causes* the town drunk.

No matter what I might say, not say, do or not do, I cannot cause anyone else to reject the faith. I may be their excuse, but I am not their cause. Not that I can let us off the hook entirely! Knowing I am surrounded by alcoholics who may be willing to enter rehab should make me cautious about sticking a drink in front of their noses—something we do all too often in the spiritual realm by being offensive, hypocritical, confusing, or condemning. I may not cause an unbeliever's addiction, but I can certainly avoid feeding it.

Stop Pulling Punches: The only hope any of us have of escaping unbelief is the freedom available through God's grace. Not only can we avoid feeding the unbeliever's addiction, but we can point them to the cure.

In his final recorded comments on earth, Jesus clearly commanded us to be his witnesses. The apostle Paul, who faced more rejection and persecution than I will ever encounter, boldly proclaimed in his letter to the Romans, "I am not ashamed of the gospel, for it is the power of God for salvation of everyone who believes." He later asked, "How can they believe in the one of whom they have not heard?" A good question.

I fear many of us become timid about proclaiming truth because we fear it will halt a supposed seeker's spiritual journey. We think that avoiding sensitive subjects, like sin, might keep the door to evangelism open. Not so. Truth comes as a package, and we must take the good with the "bad." While I must always strive to communicate in a gracious and thoughtful manner, I should be less cautious about sharing the gospel. Those determined to resist it will do so no matter how gently we present it; those eager to accept will forgive any mistakes. No one needs us to pull punches. A truly thirsty man will gratefully drink from an imperfect cup.

Start Listening: Without question, the most rewarding part of writing this book has been the time I spent with sincere unbelievers—learning their stories, hearing their objections, resonating with their doubts. For the first time in my life, I took unbelief seriously. I didn't wave it aside like an annoying fly while making my case for Christ. I did not try to argue its points, hoping instead to understand its dilemma. Malcolm Muggeridge said that to believe greatly, it's necessary to doubt greatly. If that is so, the best thing I can do to help others hear the truth is to let them talk.

I don't have all the answers. I can't defend every point of Christian theology or debunk every skeptic's attack. So why should I argue or bluff? Many of those interviewed for this book expressed how meaningful they found the dialogue, precisely because I did not try to convert them to my way of thinking. Rather than feeling accosted by faith's prosecuting attorney, they felt invited to become advocates of unbelief, to present their case in their words. In the end, some admitted finding that case less persuasive than they had assumed.

Start Early: Perhaps the most important lesson from the unconvinced to parents is to start early with our children. If unbelief is an addictive pattern that can be prevented or curtailed, then the earlier we begin teaching the truth to and modeling belief for our kids, the better. The notion that we should wait until children are old enough to "decide for themselves" is dead wrong. The Scriptures command parents to "impress them [God's words] on your children" from the earliest age, precisely because of their natural bent toward unbelief. The longer we allow them to remain in such a state, the more likely they are to remain there.

> *We will not hide them from their children; we will tell the next generation the praiseworthy deeds of the LORD, his power, and the wonders he has done. He decreed statutes for Jacob and established the law in Israel, which he commanded our forefathers to teach their children, so the next generation would know them, even the children yet to be born, and they in turn would tell their children. Then they would put their trust in God and would not forget his deeds but would keep his commands. They would not be like their forefathers—a stubborn and rebellious generation, whose hearts were not loyal to God, whose spirits were not faithful to him. (Psalm 78:4–8)*

The pattern is clear. Those generations taught to believe early are far more likely to break the pattern of rebellion. Those that aren't, perpetuate its cycle. It is no surprise that Jesus told us to become as little children if we hope to enter the kingdom of God. Children have yet to become addicted to unbelief. As a dad, I want to keep them that way.

Grief and Grace

While I wrote this book, my mother-in-law took her last breath after a long battle with Parkinson's disease. As best we can tell, she resisted the gospel to the end. We hope otherwise; we cling to the possibility, however faint, that she made a decision in the quiet of her heart while Olivia read Scriptures amid the noise of her hospital room. But in her nearly comatose state, she could not verbalize what, if anything, she thought during those final hours. We know only that a lifetime of unbelief ended, leaving us to face the grief of her death without the comforting prospect of her life beyond.

We received many sympathy cards, most senders assuming Olivia's mom died a Christian. Their words of support and affirmation, though well intentioned, felt trite. We had no assurance of the heavenly reunion they assumed. But one particular note stood out from the rest. It came from Diane, a dear friend who understood our grief as something difficult to assuage. "What you did for your mother," she wrote, "was a wonderful gift." Diane knew that Olivia had spent the prior five years making the painful transition from mother's daughter to mother's caregiver. And she knew something else. "I know what it feels like to lose an unbelieving parent."

Diane understood the sorrow, the anger, the guilt, the second-guessing, and the regrets that occur when someone you love departs this world having consistently rejected the gospel. She knew what it is to wonder what part you played in their decision to reject faith.

"Maybe I was too pushy."

"Maybe I wasn't pushy enough."

"Maybe I should have said more."

"Maybe I said too much."

Maybe. But there is no way to know, and we gain nothing by trying to figure out what we might have done wrong. It hurts to lose one we tried to love into God's arms, especially when regrets abound—such as the incident which evangelist Rambo described in chapter 7. Olivia would give anything to turn back the clock and erase the entire episode, if doing so could ensure a different outcome. But it couldn't. Among the most painful lessons I learned while listening to the unconvinced is this: whether someone accepts or rejects the gospel has little to do with what we do or avoid doing, say or neglect saying. Unbelief is not an accounting error open to audit. It is a choice that we all, God included, must allow.

What makes the difference? Exploring the reasons others give for unbelief has led me to examine my own faith decision. When so many find Christianity hard to swallow, why do I find it such a delightful dish? Why do I believe what so many reject?

I could assume I accept Christianity because my parents brought me to Sunday school as a child, rather than to a mosque or a temple or a shrine. Early training certainly makes the process easier—but not all who learn Bible stories and Jesus choruses in childhood accept the faith. Besides, many raised in a different religion later turn to Christ.

I would like to think that I accept Christianity because I am humble, willing to submit to one much greater than I. But I know myself an arrogant man.

I would like to think that I accept Christianity because I am smart, able to comprehend truths many find baffling. But I have encountered unbelievers much brighter than me.

I would like to think that I accept Christianity because I am intellectually honest, examining the evidence and reaching the only reasonable conclusion. But I first believed at seven years old, hardly mature enough to fully understand what I was doing.

I no longer consider faith in God the logical conclusion to a process of reasoning, like solving a mathematical equation. As Bishop Kallistos Ware put it, "Faith is not the supposition that something might be true, but the assurance that someone is there."[1]

The gospel of John records an incident when many disciples abandoned Jesus because they found his words hard to swallow.

> *From this time many of his disciples turned back and no longer followed him.*
> *"You do not want to leave too, do you?" Jesus asked the Twelve.*
> *Simon Peter answered him, "Lord, to whom shall we go? You have the words of eternal life. We believe and know that you are the Holy One of God." (John 6:66–69)*

I share Peter's dilemma. I do not necessarily like everything about Christianity. But I believe that God made himself known because he wants me to know him. He wants me to sense his reality through the wonders I see and the wonder that I am. I feel assured he intervenes in human affairs, from the revelation of Scripture to the incarnation of Christ to the redemption of fallen men and women like you and me. And I am convinced that he enables all of us to respond, overcoming our addictive compulsion toward rebellion with his gracious compulsion toward love.

God extended an invitation: "Whosoever will may come."

I willingly came. So he helps my unbelief. And that is why I still believe.

> *He was in the world, and though the world was made through him, the world did not recognize him. He came to that which was his own, but his own did not receive him. Yet to all who received him, to those who believed in his name, he gave the right to become children of God. (John 1:10–12)*

Notes

1. Pester the Perishing

1. Charles H. Gabriel, *Great Hymns of the Faith* (Grand Rapids, Mich.: Zondervan, 1977), 424.
2. Edward S. Ufford, *Great Hymns of the Faith*, 426.
3. Fanny Crosby, *Great Hymns of the Faith*, 432.
4. C. S. Lewis, *The Weight of Glory and Other Addresses* (New York: HarperCollins, 1976), 140.
5. Dale Ahlquist, *G. K. Chesterton—The Apostle of Common Sense* (San Francisco: Ignatius, 2003), 45.
6. Mark, Chapter 3.

2. Saint Mary Ellen

1. Donald Neal Walsh, *Conversations with God* (New York: Putnam, 1996), 36.

4. Dabblers

1. Frank McCourt, "God in America," *Life* magazine (December 1998), 64.
2. Jeremiah Creedon, "God with a Million Faces," *Utne Reader* (July/Aug. 1998), 42.
3. Douglas Coupland, *Life After God* (New York: Pocket Books, 1994), 178.
4. Ibid., 182–83.

5. Free Agent

1. *The Portable Emerson* (New York: Penguin, 1957), 157.

11. Thinking Free

1. Dan Barker, *Dear Christian* (Nontract No. 1, Dan Barker/FFRF, 1987).
2. Ibid.

13. Oh, God!

1. B. C. Johnson, *The Atheist Debaters Handbook* (New York: Prometheus, 1983), 12.
2. Ibid., 24.
3. Ibid., 14.
4. John Polkinghorne, *Belief in God in an Age of Science* (New Haven: Yale University Press, 1998), 1.
5. *Unlocking the Mystery of Life* (Illustra Media, 2002).
6. Fyodor Dostoevsky, *The Brothers Karamazov* (New York: Vintage, 1991), 243.
7. Ibid., 242–44.

14. On Edge

1. G. K. Chesterton, *The Everlasting Man* (San Francisco: Ignatius, 1925), 9–10.
2. Ibid.
3. Ben Ray Redman, *The Portable Voltaire* (New York: Penguin, 1955), 43.
4. Ibid., 195.
5. Ibid., 26.
6. Ibid.
7. Ibid., 37.
8. Friedrich Nietzsche, *Twilight of the Idols/The Anti-Christ* (New York: Penguin,1968), 58–59.
9. Ibid., 55.
10. Ibid., 64–65.
11. Ibid., 65.
12. Ibid., 99.
13. Ibid., 100.
14. Ibid., 140–41.
15. Ibid., 175.
16. Ibid., 198–99.
17. Armand M. Nicholi Jr., *The Question of God* (New York: Free Press, 2002), 55.
18. Ibid., 44.
19. Ibid., 72.
20. Ibid., 44.
21. Ernst L. Freud, *Letters of Sigmund Freud* (Questia Library), 453.
22. Bertrand Russell, *Why I Am Not a Christian* (New York: Touchstone, 1957), 14.
23. Ibid., 9.
24. Ibid., 7.

25. Ibid., 14–15.
26. Ibid., 17.
27. Ibid., 19.
28. Ibid., 21.
29. Ibid., 29–30.
30. Ibid., 44.
31. Paul Vitz, *Faith of the Fatherless* (Dallas: Spence, 1999), 5.

15. Nervous Laughter

1. Mark Twain, *Huckleberry Finn*, Chapter 3, 1–2.
2. Mark Twain, *Letters from the Earth* (New York: HarperPerennial, 1991), 7–8.
3. Ibid., 27.
4. Ibid., 49.
5. Ibid., 45.
6. Ibid., 55.
7. Linda Sunshine, ed., *The Illustrated Woody Allen Reader* (New York: Knopf, 1993).

17. The Elephant in the Room

1. *Dante's Inferno*, Canto 34.
2. C. S. Lewis, *Mere Christianity* (New York: Touchstone, 1943), 39.

18. Insanity

1. Peter Shaffer, *Amadeus* (New York: Harper & Row, 1980), 47.
2. Ibid., 49.
3. Ibid., 94.
4. John Milton, *Paradise Lost* (New York: Signet Classics, 1968), Book 1, vv. 261–63.
5. Ibid., Book 1, vv. 156–65.
6. Mark Rutland, *Behind the Glittering Mask* (Ann Arbor, Mich.: Servant, 1996), 46.
7. Ibid., 47.

19. Highway to Hell

1. Marilyn Manson, *The Long Hard Road Out of Hell* (New York: Regan, 1999), 31.
2. Ibid., 26.
3. Ibid., 164.
4. Ibid., 80.
5. Christopher Marlowe, *Dr. Faustus* (London: Dent, 1937), 34.
6. Ibid., 37.

7. Ibid., 51.
8. Ibid., 51–52.
9. Ibid., 96.
10. C. S. Lewis, *The Great Divorce* (New York: Simon & Schuster, 1946), 72.
11. Ibid., 96.
12. Manson, *Long Hard Road*, 164.

20. Recovering Unbeliever

1. Bishop Kallistos Ware, *The Orthodox Way* (New York: St. Vladimirs Seminary, 2001), 16.

Inklings of God
What Every Heart Suspects
Kurt Bruner

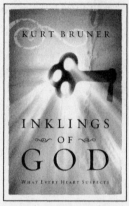

We know we are made for more. We know something is wrong. We know it needs to be set right again.

Every person is on a spiritual journey —and deep within, each of us suspects there is something more. We find hints of what we seek in the stories we tell, the wonders we create, and the religions we profess. *Inklings of God* explores the ways we find meaning in the joys and pains of everyday life, offering glimpses of someone who is with us in our searching, who is searching for us in return.

Bruner takes a fresh, provocative approach to some of the most difficult questions of human experience: How can a good God allow suffering? Why is there evil in the world? Do all religions lead to the same God? He finds answers to these burning questions in such unexpected places as laughter, music, sex, sorrow, art, science, beauty, and even death. Through it all, he shows how each moment offers an opportunity for intimate encounters with a God who is never far away.

Hardcover: 0-310-24996-1

Pick up a copy today at your favorite bookstore!

ZONDERVAN™

GRAND RAPIDS, MICHIGAN 49530 USA

WWW.ZONDERVAN.COM

We want to hear from you. Please send your comments about this
book to us in care of zreview@zondervan.com. Thank you.

GRAND RAPIDS, MICHIGAN 49530 USA

WWW.ZONDERVAN.COM